The Castles of Glamorgan

Other titles in the Monuments in the Landscape series

Monuments in the Landscape

Volume XII

The Castles of Glamorgan

by
Lise Hull

Logaston Press

LOGASTON PRESS
Little Logaston Woonton Almeley
Herefordshire HR3 6QH
logastonpress.co.uk

First published by Logaston Press 2007
Copyright © Lise Hull 2007

ISBN 978 1904396 75 8

Typeset by Logaston Press
and printed in Great Britain by
Oaklands Book Services Ltd., Gloucestershire

Contents

Please Note

Many of the monuments mentioned in this book are on private land and permission from the owner must be obtained before visiting them. Most, however, can be seen from adjacent roads or footpaths.

The following points should also be observed:

1. When visiting sites in the countryside, always follow the Countryside Code.
2. On all sites, extreme care should be taken.
3. Any artefacts found on sites should be reported to the nearest museum.
4. Under no circumstances should visitors dig in or around any site. Any damage could result in prosecution.
5. It is an offence under the 1979 Ancient Monuments and Archaeological Areas Act to use metal detectors on or near scheduled ancient monuments. In addition, simple 'treasure hunting' near ancient monuments can damage evidence to such an extent that archaeologists are unable to interpret it fully in the future.

Acknowledgments

During my studies at the University of Wales in Aberystwyth, I had the good fortune to do my placement at the Royal Commission on the Ancient and Historical Monuments of Wales. The experience was enlightening; the wealth of resources astounding. Two of their weighty tomes, *The Early Castles of Glamorgan* and *The Later Castles of Glamorgan*, became the backbone for my research for this book. I highly recommend that anyone doing scholarly research on the castles of Glamorgan seek out these massive studies.

I have explored the majority of the castles featured in this book. Many of my site descriptions vary from the Royal Commission's, due to recent consolidation or excavation, and, even more so, due to temperamental weather conditions, roving livestock and burrowing wildlife, quarrying, and commercial development, among other activities. I hope you will find *The Castles of Glamorganshire* a helpful, easy-to-use and easy-to-understand guide that is portable and can be used both when visiting the sites in person and for your own research purposes.

As always, John Kenyon has provided invaluable guidance and suggestions for my research. I thank him for letting me pick his brain.

I would also like to thank Terry Breverton, who is based in the Vale of Glamorgan, for encouraging me to do this project in the first place; and Katy Shoesmith for drawing the castle plans.

And, once again, Andy Johnson at Logaston Press has made the process of writing and publishing this book an enjoyable, comfortable and educational venture. His steadfast enthusiasm and willingness to seek out the castles I could not personally visit have helped make this book as accurate and up-to-date as possible. Any errors, however, are mine.

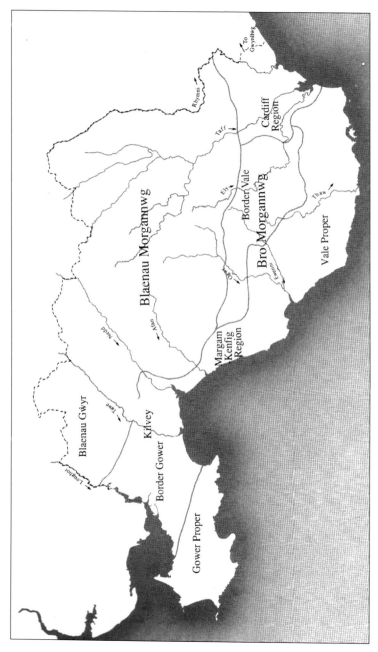

Map showing the area covered by the book and the medieval territories mentioned

Author's Introduction

You don't have to look far in the Welsh countryside to find some relic of the past, a past that shaped the social, political, and cultural identities of every part of modern-day Wales. From prehistoric cairns to Roman-era forts, from medieval farmsteads to Victorian dock-lands, from the mines to the chapels, every feature in the landscape demonstrates in a very physical way how humankind impacted the face of Wales. During the Middle Ages, the landscape was gradually, sometimes forcibly, taken over by the Normans, outsiders who constructed fortresses which both physically and symbolically subdued the local populace. The Welsh response was often harsh, sometimes acquiescent. Over time, the cultures blended, but neither completely disappeared from Wales.

In many ways, the history of Glamorganshire typifies what happened throughout Wales after the Norman Conquest. The Normans gradually pushed westward from England into South Wales, assimilating very few Welsh along the way. Most were forced into the fringes of Glamorgan: upland, isolated areas underlain by coal fields where the Normans preferred not to live. Opting for the more fertile, lowland areas, the Normans settled southern Glamorgan and took over the Gower Peninsula. There, they founded castles and manorial estates, established churches and monastic communities, and possessed the power of minor kings.

Between the 11th and 14th centuries, scores of castles were constructed in Glamorganshire. Their builders quarried local stone, reshaped hillsides, and intruded into the landscape, creating defensive strongholds which at least temporarily controlled the region. Welsh-built castles, which were generally less powerfully built, could rarely compete with the more formidable Anglo-Norman fortresses; instead, the Welsh relied upon their historical familiarity with the inhospitable landscape, known as the Blaenau Morgannwg, for shelter and refuge. From there, they staged forays into Bro Morgannwg, the Normanised lowland areas, and relentlessly resisted outside domination.

From the simplest ringwork to the most complex concentric fortress, the castles of Glamorganshire represent the entire history of castle-building in Britain. Each played a role in the development of South Wales, and of Wales as a nation. Their presence in the landscape is a constant reminder of the forces that shaped Wales and influenced Welsh identity. While castles may be an ever-present reminder of the subjugation that came with conquest, they also endure as everlasting testimonies to the power of Welsh resistance and resilience in the face of adversity. That the structures still stand, albeit in ruin, indicates just how skilful their builders were. That the invaders erected so many increasingly complex fortresses clearly demonstrates just how formidable a foe the Welsh could be.

I Early Castles in Glamorganshire

Before the 10th century, control of south-eastern Wales mainly belonged to two kingdoms, Gwent and Glywysing. Then, in the 10th century, after the death of his brother Cadwgan, Morgan ab Owain of Glywysing gained control of the area. He swiftly consolidated it into one kingdom, Morgannwg, and renamed the portion roughly corresponding with Bro Morgannwg as 'Gwlad Morgan'. Despite the creation of the new kingdom, Morgannwg was actually comprised of a grouping of many sub-kingdoms.

From 1055 to 1063, both Morgannwg and Gwent were controlled by Gruffydd ap Llywelyn, of the House of Gwynedd, the first native Welshman to rule all of Wales. An ambitious, and some say malicious, man, Gruffydd's takeover of Wales began in about 1039, when he overthrew Iago ab Idwal and ousted his son, Cynan, from Gwynedd. From then until he completed his consolidation of Wales with the seizure of Morgannwg in 1057, Gruffydd gradually defeated the native kingdoms, beginning with Deheubarth, his key rival. In 1045, Gruffydd ap Rhydderch ab Iestyn and his brother Rhys became the rulers of Morgannwg. They too wanted to control Deheubarth and managed to do just that in 1047, when they attacked and defeated Gruffydd ap Llywelyn. They apparently left Morgannwg in the hands of the rightful heirs to the lordship, Meurig ap Hywel (1045-1055) and his son, Cadwgan ap Meurig (1045-1074), and they ruled jointly for a time. In 1057, Gruffydd ap Llywelyn forced Cadwgan out of Wales and became its sole leader.

Yet, Gruffydd was not content merely with controlling Wales. In fact, he had already started campaigns in England to expand his

1

powerbase. His alliance with Aelfgar of Mercia in 1055 not only led his marriage with Ealdgyth, Aelfgar's daughter, but also to the capture of Whitford, Hope, Bangor Is-coed, Chirk, Presteigne, and Radnor, all of which were located in the Welsh Marches. And, perhaps most importantly, the allies stormed and looted Hereford, burned its castle and cathedral, and disgraced the Anglo-Saxon defenders. Clearly, Gruffydd was a man not to be trifled with.

It took six years before the Saxons mounted their revenge against the Welshman. None other than Harold Godwinsson, the future King Harold II, and his brother Tostig staged a massive effort by land and sea which resulted in Gruffydd's defeat in Snowdonia, and also the Welsh king's death and dismemberment. Ironically, Gruffydd ap Llywelyn's killers were his own men. Three years later, in 1066, Harold married Ealdgyth, Gruffydd ap Llywelyn's widow, an act that reiterated Anglo-Saxon supremacy over the Welsh. Shortly thereafter, Godwinsson became Harold II, King of England, after the death of Edward the Confessor. That death, of course, precipitated Duke William of Normandy's invasion and the death of Harold II at the Battle of Hastings.

After Gruffydd's death, Wales fractioned once again into a series of separate territories ruled by individual leaders. Gwynedd and Powys passed to Gruffydd's half-brothers, Bleddyn and Rhiwallen; Caradog ap Gruffydd seized Gwent and Gwynllwg; and Cadwgan ap Meurig regained control of Morgannwg. In 1074, Caradog seized Morgannwg from Cadwgan, but his rule ended at Mynydd Carn at the hands of Rhys ap Tewdwr, Prince of Deheubarth, in 1081. For all practical purposes, after the Battle of Mynydd Carn, Rhys ap Tewdwr controlled all of Wales; yet, in reality, the conflicts that continued between the native princes cost his considerable power. That same year, Iestyn ap Gwrgant assumed control of Morgannwg, and held it until the Normans intruded into the area in about 1093. Speculation exists that Robert Fitzhamon himself actually killed Iestyn as the Normans made their way across southern Wales. Iestyn was the last native ruler of Morgannwg.

The Norman take-over of Glamorganshire was never fully documented, so most of what we know comes from interpreting the historical record. The Normans in fact did not 'conquer'

Glamorgan. Rather, after 1066, they progressively, and tactically, moved into South Wales, at first ingratiating themselves with the local leaders and, ultimately, seizing lands belonging to hereditary Welsh lords and building castles. The first recorded account of Normans in the region dates to 1072, when Caradog ap Gruffydd, Prince of Gwynllwg, requested their support against Maredudd ab Owain, Prince of Deheubarth, during at battle near River Rumney (Rhymni). By this time, the kingship of Morgannwg, which Caradog ap Gruffydd commanded, extended from the River Tawe in the west to the Usk in the east. Then, in 1081, Rhys ap Tewdwr, Prince of Deheubarth, killed Caradog during the Battle of Mynydd Carn, which left southeastern Wales primed for a new leader. Rhys soon established himself as one of Wales' most formidable rulers and wielded considerable power – at least with the Normans, until they slew him in 1093. By then, the native Welsh princes had chipped away at Rhys' power base throughout Wales, including in his native Deheubarth, and his authority over them had waned.

The Normans soon completed their movement into south-eastern Wales. In 1093, William II (Rufus) placed one of his key supporters, Robert Fitzhamon, in control of Gwynllwg and Glamorgan, which Iestyn ap Gwrgant still held. During Fitzhamon's tenure, the lordship of Glamorgan extended roughly from the River Usk in the east to the River Ogmore in the west. Gwynllwg remained a separate Norman lordship, which Fitzhamon administered from Newport Castle. According to some accounts (now viewed as legend), Fitzhamon retained for himself the demesne manor of Roath and Leckwith and also Llantwit and parcelled out the remaining portions of his newly acquired lordship to 12 of his most devoted followers. In return, the men offered military service and attended a monthly court ('comitatus') held at Cardiff Castle. In 1105, Fitzhamon received a mortal wound at the Battle of Falaise, where he was speared in the head. He lingered in agony until his death in 1107; he was buried in Tewkesbury Abbey. Shortly thereafter, the lordship of Glamorgan reverted to the monarchy, and it remained in royal custody for the next six years.

Robert FitzRoy, Henry I's bastard son, became the Lord of Glamorgan when he married Mabel Fitzhamon in about 1113. Also known as Robert of Caen (or Robert FitzHenry), Fitzroy expanded the lordship of Glamorgan to encompass the lands between the Rumney (Rhymni) on the east and the River Neath (Nedd) on the west (which once formed the Welsh kingdom of Glywysing) and also the territory stretching from the Bristol Channel on the south to Breconshire on the north.

During the reign of Henry I, the Normans extended the lordship westward to the River Tawe. At Henry's death in 1135, they had a firm grip on lowland Glamorgan and the Gower Peninsula, having pushed the Welsh into the remote upland zone of Blaenau Morgannwg. In addition to the lordship of Afan, the Welsh continued to hold the upland lordships of Nedd (Neath) and Senghennydd, on Glamorgan's eastern border. During the Anarchy, FitzRoy supported King Stephen, but in 1138 he switched his allegiance to Empress Matilda. He died in 1147, shortly after founding Margam Abbey, also in Glamorgan, and is buried at St. James Priory, in Bristol, which he founded in 1137 as a Benedictine cell of Tewkesbury Abbey.

As in Glamorgan, the more fertile Gower lowlands remained the provenance of Norman overlords, who squeezed the Welsh into the rugged uplands. Founded in about 1107, the lordship of Gower extended Norman control from the River Neath westward to the River Loughor to include the entire Gower Peninsula and lands reaching northward almost to Ammanford. Henry II appointed Henry de Beaumont, Earl of Warwick, as the first Lord of Gower. Swansea served as the lordship's caput, or administrative centre. The two lordships in Glamorganshire remained separate entities until the 16th century, when Henry VIII used the Act of Union to officially unite them into a single county.

The fertile lowland areas of the Vale of Glamorgan (Bro Morgannwg) became the mainstay of the lordship and contained Glamorgan's most important castles. In addition, with 28 identified ringwork castles and another nine possible ringworks, Glamorgan also featured the highest concentration of this type of earth and timber fortification in Wales. In fact, Glamorganshire itself has more ringworks than motte castles. All of the ringworks were constructed either in the Vale of Glamorgan or near the southern coast of the

Gower, where geological conditions in these lowland areas precluded the construction of mottes. In northern upland areas, the presence of glacial ridges, which could be easily reshaped into defensive mounds, accommodated the construction of mottes. Some ringworks also incorporated glacial drift; however, most were erected in low-lying areas underlain by limestone, where glacial deposits did not exist. Several ringworks were transformed over time into substantial stone strongholds, as at Coity and Ogmore; many others were never refortified with stone.

Even though the Welsh were by no means prolific castle-builders, they probably erected the small motte castle at Gelligaer (near a Roman fort) and were most likely responsible for the possible castle sites at Briton Ferry (Hen Gastell), Castell Nos (Aberdare), Llangewydd, Oldcastle (near Bridgend), and Castell Bolan (or Cwm Clais), near Baglan. Of Glamorgan's ringworks, only two – Llanilid and Gwern-y-Domen – may be Welsh-built; however, this theory remains unsubstantiated.

Largely built between 1200 and 1325 and resembling ringworks in design, Glamorgan's moated sites became more common as the construction of new earthwork castles waned. However, at least 19 moated sites were erected prior to 1200. Of the 114 moated sites firmly dated in Wales, Glamorgan has 13 definite and four possible sites, all of which are essentially rectangular in shape. Gower, on the other hand, has no moated sites. Most had Anglo-Norman owners and were directly associated with manorial centres. Some functioned as ecclesiastical centres, while others were used for hunting lodges or supported minor structures, such as dovecotes. Many were located within sight or walking distance of a church and castle complex. Gadlys moated site, for example, sits near Llanilid, where a fine medieval church and ringwork castle stand together in a tree-clad spot. Horseland moated site was built close to the ringwork and church at Llantrithyd. Centuries later, a fine manor house was also constructed nearby.

Today, few moated sites retain any traces of the manor houses or the other structures they may have supported. The Royal Commission speculates that these sites may have fit the needs of lesser lords, who could not afford the expense of replacing their earth and timber castles with stone but who still wanted a place to display their status. They were never meant as fortified structures.

Feudal obligations

The knight's fee was the backbone of the feudal system in medieval Britain. Believed to have been introduced by William the Conqueror, feudalism was a shrewdly devised political system of exchange and obligation, whereby the king's vassals (favoured supporters, particularly those who had a key role in the overall success of the Norman invasion) paid homage and swore fealty to the king in exchange for grants of parcels of land, known as fiefs or fees. Their feudal obligation, however, extended well beyond a simple exchange of land for lip service. The vassals owed military service to the king, both personally participating in the army as well as supplying a specific number of 'knights', together with an obligation to provide 'soldiers' to garrison a castle, often in peacetime. This latter service was known as 'castle-guard' or 'castle ward'. Some vassals owed alternate forms of service, such as sergeantry, for example, whereby they provided the use of their lands for the king's hunts.

The process that became known as 'sub-infeudation' further subdivided the landscape into smaller parcels. The greater vassals would grant portions of their holdings to lesser lords or tenants while retaining a portion (the demesne) for their own purposes. In return, the lesser vassals owed their lord knight service or castle-guard duty. The basic unit of feudal land, the fief, was also known as a fee or knight's fee. A single knight's fee could, in theory, support the needs of a horseman while serving his feudal obligation. Some vassals owed service only during wartime, whereas others performed their obligations over the course of a year. The exact number (or quota) of men expected from a lord was determined by a number of factors, such as the size of the lordship, the wealth of the lord and the value of the land he controlled. Inconsistent and often resisted, the quota system turned out to be a relatively inefficient way to recruit troops; consequently, the king or greater lord used other methods to pull in soldiers when required.

As early as the reign of Henry II, in the late 12th century, many fief-holders began paying off their feudal obligation with money rather than military service, most often substituting cash or another form of payment for castle duty. The payment, known as scutage, might be used to hire mercenary soldiers to garrison a castle or to fight for the lord or king who had paid for their services. During wartime, the king would issue a feudal summons, which called all men owing knight's service to gather. In these situations, feudal obligations were primarily paid in person.

During the 13th century, Henry III relied upon the heavy enforcement of feudal service to man his armies against the barons during their protracted uprising against the Crown, including at the siege of Kenilworth Castle in 1266, which lasted nine months (see also under Caerphilly Castle in the gazetteer).

A contemporary representation of Henry III

Kings Edward I and Edward II routinely issued feudal summonses, but increasingly resorted to the payment of scutage to maintain their armies in England. In Scotland and Ireland, personal military service continued to be relied upon well into the 14th century, and even later. In 1327, Edward III issued a single feudal summons; afterwards, these orders essentially became obsolete. In 1344, however, Edward III did attempt to create a new system of military obligation, whereby he assessed individual men whose income was more than £5 per year and required them to provide a number of soldiers based upon that income. The policy created a great deal of discontent, and, in 1352, the king agreed that no one should be required to fulfill his feudal obligation with military service. The agreement rang the death knell for feudalism. The final feudal summons was issued in 1385. In the 1660s, during the Restoration, the system of feudal obligation was abolished altogether.

The Transition to Stone

Although the construction of earthwork castles waned as the need for more formidable defences increased over time, many were occupied well into the late Middle Ages. However, almost immediately after their completion, owners replaced the timber ramparts, which were susceptible to rot, battering and burning, with stone fortifications. The need for sturdier defences coupled with the rising status of the minor lords led to renewed building efforts at many sites. Interestingly, whereas the majority of motte castles were never converted to stone, most of the region's ringworks received masonry fortifications, including substantial stone keeps and faceted curtain walls. In fact, Glamorganshire actually contains the highest concentration of rectangular stone keeps in Wales, the earliest of which dates to 1125 and survives in ruin alongside the main gateway into the inner ward of the ringwork castle at Ogmore.

Generally, the plans of Glamorgan's 12th-century stone castles reflected the layouts of the original earthen fortifications at the sites, which owners strengthened with masonry, an enclosing curtain wall, and a keep. Examples include the major lordship castles at Cardiff and Swansea. Many of the castles that served the minor lordships, including those reputedly established by Robert Fitzhamon, also acquired stone defences. The Normans built rectangular keeps adjacent to the entrances of ringworks (Ogmore), placed them in the inner ward immediately opposite the main gateway (Newcastle Bridgend), or embedded them in the curtain wall some distance from the entrance (Dinas Powys).

Payn de Turberville II (d.1207) initiated the first masonry construction at Coity Castle, when he replaced his grandfather's timber ramparts with a faceted curtain wall and added the keep to the north-west side of the inner ward. Located near Bridgend and Ogmore, the castle's refortification may have come in response to increasing tension with the Welsh, who revolted shortly after William FitzRobert, Lord of Glamorgan, died in 1183. Or, Payn II may have decided to strengthen the castle in 1189 after John, the new English king, granted neighbouring Newcastle Bridgend to Morgan ap Caradog, Lord of Afan, who had led the uprising six years earlier.

Initially erected in the late 12th century, de Turberville's keep rose three storeys; another level was added in the 16th century, when the adjoining annexe was also heightened. The earliest masonry at Coity Castle can easily be detected by its red colouration, the result of combining blocks of local red conglomerate with red mortar to fill the core of the walls. Grey Sutton stone quoins added an element of ornamentation. Placed immediately to the left of the main entry point into the inner ward, as at Ogmore and Newcastle, Coity's rectangular keep is now almost completely ruined. Enough survives, however, to provide an impression of the building's medieval appearance.

By the late 12th century, a rectangular stone keep – the largest of its kind in Glamorgan – dominated Kenfig Castle. Historians once believed Iestyn ap Gwrgant erected a motte castle at the site in about 1080, but now most accept that Robert FitzRoy built the original stronghold in the early 12th century. With its layout comparable to that at Newcastle Bridgend, it seems likely that the first Kenfig Castle may also have begun as a ringwork. Dispute arises when one considers that the castle was situated on a low-lying glacial ridge, a factor some would argue indicates a greater likelihood that FitzRoy erected a motte here. Unfortunately, no evidence of the earthwork castle survives to substantiate either theory.

Kenfig Castle was designed as an almost circular enclosure with a freestanding keep positioned directly opposite the main entrance. Excavations conducted in the 1920s revealed the use of Carboniferous limestone, Pennant stone and glacial pebbles, as well as Roman-era tile and brick, to form the walls' rubble core. Skilfully-cut ashlar provided the exterior facing. The discovery of an ornate Norman-era capital suggests that a fine hall occupied the first floor of the keep. During the mid-13th century, two arrowslits were cut into the walls at ground level and a latrine tower was added to the north-western corner.

Other ringworks that acquired masonry defences include Barry, Llanblethian, Llantrisant, Neath, Pennard, Penmark, Penrice, Rumney, St. Donats, Sully, and Talyfan.

Interestingly, only one masonry castle in Glamorgan – Plas Baglan – has been reliably identified as Welsh-built. Located near Baglan, the simple stronghold consisted of a square walled enclosure with a rectangular hall or square tower in one corner. It was probably built by Morgan ap Caradog in the late 12th century to replace the motte at nearby Aberafan. The Welsh may also have built Castell Morgraig. Some historians believe the de Clares constructed the castle as a border stronghold to hold back the Welsh; however, others have provided ample evidence that the castle was begun in the mid-13th century either by Llywelyn ap Gruffydd or Gruffydd ap Rhys and that Gilbert de Clare subsequently modified it.

II   Politics and the Apogee of Castle building in Glamorganshire

Despite arranged marriages intended to keep the peace, the Welsh lords of Senghennydd, Afan, Meisgyn, Machen, and Gwynllwg became increasingly intolerant of the losses they had incurred at the hands of the Lords of Glamorgan and Gower during the 13th century. Their actions sparked a series of rebellions, not just in Glamorganshire but throughout Wales. Not only did Llywelyn ab Iorwerth, Prince of Gwynedd, make his way to southern Wales, rallying forces along the way, but regional Welsh lords, such as Rhys Ieuanc and Rhys Gryg, also began torching towns and assaulting castles in an effort to oust the Anglo-Norman lords, who had begun merging the Welsh upland commotes with their lordships.

In 1212, Rhys Gryg and Maelgwyn, sons of the Lord Rhys, Prince of Deheubarth, attacked and burned Swansea and the castle, but the latter remained the property of the Lord of Gower. Three years later, the heir to the lordship of Senghennydd, Rhys Ieuanc (also known as Rhys ap Gruffydd) assaulted the lordship of Gower, then under the control of William Marshal, Earl of Pembroke, seizing all the castles and again attacking Swansea. (Rhys Ieuanc also briefly held Loughor Castle and captured and destroyed Castell Talybont during Llywelyn ab Iorwerth's rebellion against Henry III. Nonetheless, the English soon regained control of both sites.) The garrison at Swansea reputedly set torch to the neighbouring borough in order to properly defend the castle, but accounts of the event indicate that the Welsh probably seized the stronghold. Control of Swansea vacillated between the Welsh and the Lord of Gower. In 1216, Llywelyn

Part of the Buck brothers' view of Swansea showing what still remained of the, much rebuilt, castle in 1741

granted the lordship to Reginald de Braose, who had married the Welshman's daughter, Gwladus Ddu.

By 1217, the Welsh had ousted the Anglo-Norman lords from Gower, ravaged the countryside, and destroyed Swansea Castle. Rhys Gryg claimed the lordship of Gower from de Braose, except for Kilvey and Landimore, which Morgan Gam retained. Then, in 1218, several Welsh lords, including Morgan Gam (of Afan) and Hywel ap Maredudd (of Meisgyn), declared their independence from Glamorgan. As fate would have it, when Llywelyn ab Iorwerth finally settled his differences with Henry III, Rhys Gryg refused to pay homage to the king. Instead, he set about evicting the English once again from the Gower, ravaging Swansea Castle in the process. So, in 1220, Llywelyn ousted his countryman from the lordship and granted Swansea Castle to John de Braose, who immediately repaired and refortified the stronghold with stone.

Even so, the presence of masonry defences at Swansea failed to deter the Welsh. In 1257, under the leadership of Llywelyn ap

Gruffydd and Rhys Fychan (Lord of Dinefwr), they again attacked the Gower and burned Swansea, inflicting minor damage to the castle but failing to seize it from the Lord of Gower. In 1287, Rhys ap Maredudd and the Welsh again stormed the Gower, attacked Swansea Castle and briefly captured Oystermouth Castle.

Kenfig Castle and its adjoining borough also experienced the wrath of the Welsh. Attacks occurred in 1167; 1183-84 (led by Morgan ap Caradog); 1228 (led by Hywel ap Maredudd); 1232 (led by Morgan Gam); 1243 (led by Hywel ap Maredudd); 1295 (led by Morgan ap Maredudd); and 1316 (possibly led by Llywelyn Bren). On each occasion, the borough was burned or destroyed, but the only time the Welsh inflicted serious damage on the castle occurred during the assault in 1295.

In 1322, the lordship of Gower reverted to the Crown after the execution of William de Braose III (then Lord of Gower) for his role in the Battle of Boroughbridge, which took place near York. During the battle Edward II's army, led by Sir Andrew de Harcla, defeated rebelling forces led by his cousin, Thomas, Earl of Lancaster (Lancaster had played a key role in the murder of Piers Gaveston, the king's favourite, in 1311). Edward II then granted the lordship to Hugh le Despenser, another favourite, who was also Lord of Glamorgan. Before exchanging his castles with Elizabeth (de Clare) Damory for castles in the lordships of Caerleon, Usk and Trelleck, Despenser plundered the lordship of Gower and devastated several castles. From then onwards, ownership of the Gower castles alternated between the de Braoses, de Mowbrays, the Earls of Warwick and Nottingham, the Herberts of Raglan, and the monarchy. As absentee lords, they focused little attention on the lordship and its castles, and, with the exception of Swansea, the Gower castles began to decay.

The de Clare Legacy
The 13th and 14th centuries marked the heyday of castle-building in Glamorganshire as Welsh insurgency began to grip southern Wales. In 1217, the de Clares assumed the lordship of Glamorgan.

Besides making modifications to extant strongholds, the de Clares also erected six new castles from scratch and introduced several important design innovations: the round tower, the twin-towered gatehouse, and the concentric design. In 1246, Richard de Clare installed round keeps at Llantrisant and Talyfan castles, and, 42 years later, Gilbert de Clare II added two massive round towers/keeps to Morlais Castle. Rectangular keeps were also built at Morgraig and Loughor castles. In all, by the late 13th century, 26 stone castles dominated Glamorgan; another seven masonry strongholds appeared in the Gower lordship, where landscape conditions and poor quality materials forced builders to construct less substantial castles than they could raise in Glamorgan.

Rebellions riddled Glamorgan in 1224, 1226, 1228-29, and in 1233-34. During 1242-43, Hywel ap Maredudd, Rhys Ieuanc, and their Welsh followers assaulted Coity and Kenfig, among other sites. In 1247, after de Clare instituted a policy of annexation, consolidation, and the imposition of feudal authority, Welsh resistance continued sporadically for a time.

Llantrisant Castle's tumultuous history, for example, was marked by frequent assaults followed by periods of rebuilding. During the 13th and 14th centuries, the castle was repeatedly targeted by the Welsh, who resented the power held by both Richard de Clare and his son, Gilbert, and also their successor, Hugh le Despenser. The Welsh ravaged the borough in about 1258; the castle was probably also assaulted, but no record survives of that event. Madog ap Llywelyn (of Machen and Caerleon) and his compatriot, Morgan ap Maredudd (rightful heir to Gwynllwg), conducted the next major onslaught at Llantrisant in 1294-1295, which devastated the castle and probably also destroyed the borough. Another period of rebuilding failed to prevent additional attacks, and the Welsh revolts of 1314 and 1316 caused further devastation at Llantrisant.

In 1267, Gilbert de Clare II effectively completed the unification of the upland Welsh-held territories with the lowland, Norman-dominated portions of Glamorgan, seizing Is Caeach, the lower portion of Senghennydd. He sealed his position with the construction of Caerphilly Castle, arguably Wales' finest fortress. However, despite a temporary truce instituted in late 1268, the issue of land ownership between the Welsh and the Lord of Glamorgan remained unresolved. In October 1270, Llywelyn ap Gruffydd launched yet another assault on Glamorgan, ravaging the castle at Caerphilly and forcing de Clare to begin a new construction programme. Henry III attempted to settle the dispute, but when Prince Edward (the future King Edward I) granted Llywelyn lands that had belonged to de Clare, the enraged Lord of Glamorgan remained defiant. In 1271, de Clare agreed to stop construction at Caerphilly Castle so that he did not have an unfair advantage over the Welsh prince while the lands issue remained unsettled. However, de Clare's acquiescence was merely a bid for more time to plan his next move.

In February 1272, de Clare successfully reclaimed control of Caerphilly Castle with a shrewd act of deception. When the constable of Cardiff Castle and two soldiers entered the castle to inventory its supplies, they deliberately left the gates open so that the other 40 soldiers who had accompanied them could rush inside. Because the king could not prove de Clare's duplicity in this seizure, he relinquished control of the castle to the Lord of Glamorgan. With this action, Llywelyn ap Gruffydd gave up Welsh claims to lands in the region.

Even though rebellion continued to threaten Gilbert de Clare's Glamorgan, King Edward I found himself preoccupied with Llywelyn ap Gruffydd and the Welsh army in North Wales. Consequently, Caerphilly remained unscathed during the two Welsh Wars for Independence, in 1277 and 1282. The timing was fortuitous for de Clare, who could invest considerable effort and money on the building works at Caerphilly Castle. By 1278, the castle had essentially reached its full extent.

The introduction of the concentric design was certainly the most important development in the history of castle-building in Glamorgan – and in Wales – and reached its zenith at Caerphilly. Not only did Gilbert de Clare II initiate the massive building programme, which created a complex series of inner and outer wards surrounded by progressively higher towers and gatehouses, he flooded the enclosing landscape with vast lakes. De Clare also made extensive use of round towers to guard his inner ward and front his gatehouses. Such was the quality of de Clare's masterpiece that his king, Edward I, adapted the design for his mighty castles at Harlech and Beaumaris. Twin-towered gatehouses, albeit on a smaller scale than at Caerphilly, can

Caerphilly Castle as depicted on a postcard im the mid 1970s

also be found at several castles in Glamorganshire, such as Pennard and Oystermouth Castles.

With Caerphilly completed, Gilbert de Clare promptly turned his attention to his Anglo-Norman rival, Humphrey de Bohun, lord of neighbouring Brecon. Disagreement erupted over the rights to Morlais Castle, the construction of which de Clare had begun in 1288 on the edge of the lordship of Glamorgan near what is now Merthyr Tydfil, but perilously close to the border with the lordship of Brecon. The situation inevitably led to conflict, which forced the king to intervene.

Gilbert de Clare's last hurrah involved yet another Welsh rebellion, this time led by Morgan ap Maredudd, son of the former Lord of Machen. After first ravaging Morlais Castle in the summer of 1294, the Welsh rebels then marched on Caerphilly. Though the castle remained strong, they burned half of the town. Shortly thereafter the Welsh rebels successfully burned the de Clare stronghold at Llangynwyd. The following spring, when de Clare retaliated, Morgan 'surrendered to the king's peace', claiming he had no dispute with Edward I but only with the Lord of Glamorgan. Control of Tir Iarll (Earl's Land), a demesne lordship created from the upland area north of Kenfig which jutted into Blaenau Morgannwg, then shifted from Llangynwyd Castle to that at Kenfig, and Llangynwyd was abandoned and forgotten until 1906.

By the end of 1294, Gilbert de Clare II had died. Caerphilly Castle and the rest of Glamorgan passed temporarily to his widow, Joan, during the minority of their son, Gilbert III. When Gilbert III died without a male heir on the battlefield at Bannockburn in 1314, the castle and all other de Clare estates were held in limbo until Edward II finally distributed them amongst Gilbert's three sisters. Administration of Caerphilly Castle fell to appointed custodians, including Bartholomew de Badlesmere, Payn de Turberville, and William de Berkerolles, none of whom particularly impressed the Welsh. Then, Llywelyn ap Gruffydd (also known as Llywelyn Bren), whose family had been the Lords of Senghennydd, decided to claim his rightful inheritance.

Gathering some 10,000 men to his cause, Llywelyn Bren attacked Caerphilly Castle in January 1316 and seized the constable, de Berkerolles. Even though rebellion spread throughout the region, the castle yet again withstood the onslaught: only one drawbridge, probably the one fronting the south gatehouse, was destroyed. However, the town and its mills were completely devastated. Indeed, much of Glamorgan was targeted by the Welsh at this time, but Edward II's army forced their surrender in March. Llywelyn Bren, his wife, and five sons were imprisoned in the Tower of London.

The king then appointed John Giffard as the new custodian of Caerphilly Castle, but it soon passed to Hugh le Despenser the Younger in 1317 by right of marriage to Eleanor de Clare, one of Gilbert III's three sisters. One of Despenser's first acts as Lord of Glamorgan was the brutal execution of Llywelyn Bren, who was hanged, beheaded, and quartered in 1318. The killing was a key cause of the barons' rebellion against Despenser in 1321. Joining forces with the Welsh, Kenfig was attacked for an eighth time. Borough and castle were completely destroyed, as were many of Despenser's other castles in Glamorgan; but, by the end of the century, Kenfig had been rebuilt. After the executions of Despenser and his king, Edward II, in 1326 and 1327, Eleanor Despenser reacquired the lordship of Glamorgan, which passed to her new husband, William, Lord Zouche.

Ironically, the architectural innovations implemented by the de Clares during the 13th century marked the beginning of the end of castle-building in Glamorgan. Though many castles were modified and increasingly lavish structures added (like Hugh le Despenser's great hall at Caerphilly), no new castles were constructed in Glamorgan after this time. During the 14th and 15th centuries, the trend in castle design moved away from massive military fortresses that also afforded accommodation, to smaller, less fortified manor houses and tower houses.

Glamorgan's four tower houses date to the 14th and 15th centuries and were situated in fertile lowland agricultural areas at the centres of medieval manors. Two of the sites, Llandough Castle and Tythegston Court, have been incorporated into later buildings, which are still occupied. The other two, Weobley and Candleston castles, remain impressive even in ruin. The needs and fashion of the times had begun to change; while defence was still valued, it was not as visible an indicator of status as was a substantial home.

III   Castles and the Industrial Age

After the defeat of King Charles I during the Civil Wars of the mid-17th century, scores of true castles were intentionally slighted, or rendered useless, by Parliamentary troops, and castle-building effectively halted throughout the realm. Parts of some castles, particularly the gatehouses and keeps, found new uses as prisons or were leased to tenant farmers. Others fell into ruin.

The Shams

By the 16th century, the gentry class had begun to dominate South Wales. Many landowners took the opportunity their wealth afforded them to rebuild their castles and lighten the defensive features, or to build new homes on a grandiose scale. The trend escalated after the English Civil War. Some continued to call their homes 'castles', as at Oxwich and Old Beaupre, and added castellation to substantiate that claim. Others built from scratch such as Sir Thomas Morgan, steward to the Earl of Pembroke, who built the impressive structure known as Ruperra Castle in 1626. Located near the motte castle of the same name, the castellated mansion, with its battlemented towers, was restored by Thomas Hardwick in the 1780s, after a fire had ravaged the structure. Ruperra (new) Castle remained the property of the Morgans, who became Lords of Tredegar, until they sold it in 1956. By then it had become a ruin, which it remains to this day.

A resurgence of 'castle'-building occurred in the 18th century, when 'industrial feudalism' began to dominate the valleys of South Wales. Many castellated stately homes appeared around Glamorgan-

Ruperra Castle

shire, their wealthy owners calling their mansions 'castles' to emphasise the importance of their residences – and themselves. More accurately termed 'sham' castles, they were built to look like medieval castles but not to function as military structures. In reality, these buildings never met the definition of a true castle; at best, their fanciful names merely reflected their owners' aspirations and their ability to reap vast monetary rewards while their employees endured horrendous working conditions and lived in poverty.

Built in the 1820s for industrialist William Crawshay, magnificent Cyfarthfa Castle (SO 042074) is one of Glamorgan's most notable sham castles. It was deliberately positioned to overawe one of the world's largest ironworks, the products from which gave the Crawshays their fortune. Crawshay spent about £30,000 to build the home, which featured 365 windows, and to landscape the surroundings with gardens, vineyards, and greenhouses. Notable architectural features included turrets with false machicolations, circular towers, lavish interiors with ornamental chimneypieces and plasterwork, and an impressive neo-Gothic entranceway.

The Crawshays continued to live at Cyfarthfa Castle until 1909 when the local council purchased the structure. Located near Merthyr Tydfil, Cyfarthfa Castle is now a museum and art gallery. It still

Cyfarthfa Castle in the mid 1900s

overlooks a terrace of ironworkers' tiny cottages at Chapel Row, one of which is open to the public.

Other sham castles in Glamorganshire include Clyne Castle (SS 614906), Hensol Castle (ST 047789), Morris Castle (SS 659964), and Wenvoe Castle (ST 120714).

The Bute Legacy

Perhaps the most flamboyant character to impact the course of recent castle-building in Wales was John Patrick Crichton Stuart, the 3rd Marquess of Bute, whose fascination with the Middle Ages inspired him to embellish Cardiff Castle and to completely restore Castell Coch. (In neither case, however, should these castles be strictly classified as shams, for both existed in the Middle Ages and served their lords as residences and fortified military strongholds.) The Butes also renovated Caerphilly Castle.

Originally hailing from the Isle of Bute in Scotland, the Bute family courted the privileges of the upper class. Marrying wealthy heiresses, the 3rd Earl and 1st Marquess of Bute (who served as Prime Minister under King George III) and his heirs acquired enormous estates throughout Britain. John Crichton Stuart, the 2nd Marquess of Bute (also known as Lord Mountstuart), is best known as 'the Father of Modern Cardiff' for his involvement in the industrialisation of the area, the development of the coal fields in neighbouring valleys, and the construction of the docks in what became known as Butetown. He also began the restoration of Cardiff Castle. Dying in 1848, Lord Mountstuart left his enormous fortune to his infant son, John Patrick Crichton Stuart, the 3rd Marquess.

The well-educated 3rd Marquess may rightly be considered a renaissance man, but at the same time he was also very eccentric. His areas of expertise included history, heraldry, archaeology, theology, mysticism, philanthropy, and fluency in 21 languages. While studying at Oxford, Bute became increasingly interested in the Middle Ages and encountered a like-minded individual, architect William Burges. At the age of 21, the 3rd Marquess converted to Roman Catholicism from his Presbyterian upbringing; the conversion was largely influenced by his medievalist yearnings.

Having inherited Castell Coch, the 3rd Marquess eventually decided to explore the site on the south-facing hillside overlooking the River Taff. There, he discovered a jumble of ruined structures covered by undergrowth, the moat in-filled with rubble and earth. In 1871, Bute decided to restore Castell Coch (the Red Castle) and called upon his friend, William Burges, to spearhead the project. Burges was the ideal choice for this incursion into castle building. Twenty years older than Bute, Burges was an expert on medieval architecture and a true medievalist at heart who actually wore medieval attire at home. Together, the men created a castle as faithful to the original medieval structure as possible while also incorporating wildly decorated interiors.

Prior to beginning the restoration work, William Burges conducted a detailed survey and developed an elaborate plan for rebuilding Castell Coch. Partly relying on a survey completed in 1850 by G.T. Clark, who devised an accurate ground plan and shrewdly interpreted the ruins, Burges stripped out the undergrowth and rubble. Underneath, he discovered that much more of the original masonry castle existed than Clark had realised. In 1872, Burges submitted his reconstruction plan to Bute. Inside the 'Castell Coch Report', which still survives, Burges proposed to re-erect the castle as 'a country residence for occasional occupation in the summer'. In 1875, shortly after the 3rd Marquess reviewed and accepted the plan, Burges began the formidable task of transforming the ruins into a liveable residence.

To the best of his and his architect's abilities, John Patrick Crichton Stuart ensured his compact Red Castle remained true to its Norman origins, at least structurally. Inside the gatehouse (the only purely Burges structure at the castle), a working portcullis and murder holes remind visitors of the medieval need for strong defences. Like their precursors, Bute's turning bridge and portcullis were operated with a windlass, which he accurately located in the room over the gate passage. They are still in working order.

Incorporating the surviving portions of the medieval castle into his new creation, William Burges rebuilt the kitchen and keep towers with walls measuring three metres thick and sturdy spurred buttresses. He also included arrowslits, putlog holes and drainage holes, and added rectangular latrine turrets to both towers – their chutes still dump into the ditch. The well tower, on the other hand, lacks a spurred base but does contain a dungeon, reachable by stepping downwards from the wellhead inside the tower. A three-metre thick battlemented curtain wall links the well tower with the kitchen tower, as the original shell wall would have done in the 13th century. A wall-walk and embrasures with arrowslits complete the authentic appearance of what is actually a Victorian wall. Burges intended to construct a chapel on the uppermost level of the well tower, but died before it could be built.

As much as was possible, Lord Bute ensured that his master architect preserved the original masonry. That stonework consists mainly of loosely fitted light grey limestone and red sandstone rubble; it is clearly distinguishable from the later Victorian work. The modern castle features bright reddish-orange trim and towers crowned with dramatic pointed cones. Burges took his inspiration for the cones from the work of Viollet-le-Duc published in *Architecture Militaire* (1854) and in *Dictionnaire* (1854-65), creatively modelling the turrets at Castell Coch after the Frenchman's design. Burges tipped each tower with red roof-tiles styled after a medieval tile found in the rubble; in 1972, they were replaced with drab green tiles.

By 1879, the new Castell Coch was virtually complete. Interestingly, G.T. Clark closely followed the progress of the massive building programme and amended his original report when it was reprinted in 1884 to reflect the restoration work undertaken by Bute and Burges.

The Butes also left their mark at Cardiff Castle, where the Victorian flamboyance tends to overwhelm its medieval precursor, the great motte castle in the inner ward. John, the 1st Marquess of Bute (Lord Mountstuart), began his rebuilding programme immediately after acquiring the castle in 1776, hiring Lancelot 'Capability' Brown, the highly acclaimed landscape designer, to carry out the transformation. Brown tore out several structures, including the cross-wall that linked the Black Tower to the keep and the forebuilding built by the de Clares. He also demolished the remains of the medieval shire hall and the knights' houses, in-filled the moat around the motte, and redesigned the castle grounds.

The Butes first hired architect Henry Holland to remodel the western apartments. Holland gave symmetry to the residential range by extending the building to the north and adding a tower to provide balance with the southern tower, previously built by Henry Herbert. However, to accommodate the wishes of the 3rd Marquess in the late 19th century, William Burges almost completely replaced Holland's work.

The Bute legacy best reveals its medieval self at nearby Caerphilly Castle. Even though his attention was largely focussed at Cardiff Castle and Castell Coch, John Patrick Crichton Stuart also began a programme of restoration at the heavily ruined Caerphilly Castle during the 1870s. He reroofed Hugh le Despenser's great hall and ordered architect William Frame, who worked on the Bute properties in Scotland and the Bute pier head in Cardiff, to completely document the remains; Frame's drawings and plans still survive.

John Crichton Stuart, the 4th Marquess of Bute, acquired possession of Caerphilly Castle after his father's death in 1900. From 1928 to 1939, he continued his father's project and painstakingly restored the castle as authentically as possible, largely consolidating the site rather than rebuilding it. In 1950, Caerphilly Castle passed to the State, which reflooded the lakes and consolidated more masonry. It remains, in the author's opinion, Wales' greatest fortress.

Aberafan

The enormous industrial complex of Port Talbot now occupies the site where Aberafan Castle once stood. Although it served as the original centre of Port Talbot, Aberafan fell victim to the Industrial Revolution, and the castle was torn down in 1895 when an area of housing was built. Nothing survives of this perplexing site, which, from all accounts, looked more like a moated site than a motte castle. However, it has also been classified as a motte, based primarily on evidence taken from 19th-century Ordnance Survey maps and tithe schedules, which labelled the site as 'Beili y Castell', 'Baily'r Castell', and 'Bailey Castell'.

No one can now substantiate whether it was a motte castle or a moated site. According to the Royal Commission, the tiny mound in the centre of the site actually supported a cockpit; however, Salter states that the mound may have covered the remains of a stone keep. Little of the castle's medieval history survives; most records date to the 18th and 19th centuries by when only stone foundations still remained.

Close inspection of the 1876 OS map reveals a rectangular enclosure, measuring about 55 metres by 49 metres, surrounded by a dry ditch and in the centre of which is an unditched mound. The Royal Commission theorises that the enclosure actually functioned as a bailey and would have been associated with a large adjacent motte, reported by visitors in the 19th century to have been topped with stone. If that were the case, it makes some sense that the low mound inside the enclosure served as a cockpit mound rather than a motte.

During the 12th century, Aberafan Castle was a significant, albeit minor, castle. Commanding the vital communications route formed by the Rivers Neath (Nedd) and Afan and the former Roman road, the *Via Maritima*, the castle stood in a strategically valuable location close to where the River Afan flowed into Swansea Bay. The actual founder of Aberafan Castle is not known, but historians speculate that, since the Welsh retained control of the region in the decades

25

immediately after the Normans moved into Glamorgan, it is possible that Caradog ab Iestyn erected the earthen castle in the late 11th or early 12th century. However, it is known that two other Welshmen, Rhys ap Gruffydd and Maredudd, his brother (Caradog's uncles), destroyed the castle in 1153, an act that seems more reasonable if the lordship was Norman rather than Welsh at that time. The lands at Aberafan may have been the property of the Norman William FitzHenry, as was the Chapel of St. Thomas which he granted to Tewkesbury Abbey. Even though little is known about FitzHenry, speculation is that he may have been Earl Robert FitzRoy's brother, and, hence, another illegitimate son of Henry II.

After 1153, the Welsh controlled Aberafan, but from the 12th to the 14th centuries, they located their main power base at Plas Baglan, now on the opposite side of the M4 motorway, just a couple of miles to the north-west. In the late 13th century, they moved back to Aberafan and by 1304 established a small borough near the castle. At about the same time, they also fortified the castle site with masonry.

By the time Leland visited Aberafan in the 1530s, the castle had fallen into ruin. Remnants survived until 1895, when the entire site was cleared for houses and a lengthy section of masonry unearthed. The neighbouring roadway, Castle Street, marks the historic location, just west of St. Mary's parish church, which was completely rebuilt in the 19th century.

Barry

Ruins of 13th- and 14th-century inner ward and gatehouse
Location: On Park Road (ST 101 672)
Access: Freely accessible

Barry Castle lies near the ridge of the hill on the residential Park Road, itself two roads north of a park that is north of Barry Station at the west end of town.

Barry Castle once commanded an expansive view of the countryside all the way to the Bristol Channel. A Norman sub-manor existed at Barry as early as the 12th century, when it was held by the de Barri family as one of four knight's fees in the lordship of Penmark, which the Umfravilles controlled. The family adopted the name de Barri when they settled near Barry Island, which was named after the Celtic St. Barruc. Perhaps the best source for information on the de Barri history comes from one of the family's most prominent members, Gerald de Barri, also known as Gerald of Wales or Giraldus Cambrensis. Gerald's family also owned Manorbier Castle, in Pembrokeshire, where Gerald himself was born. He documented the establishment of the de Barri lineage in his two books, *The Journey through Wales* and *Description of Wales*.

The present ruins at Barry date to no earlier than the 13th century, but it is likely that an earth and timber stronghold stood on the spot by the early 12th century. Archaeological interpretation of the site during excavations in 1960 and 1979, coupled with the discovery

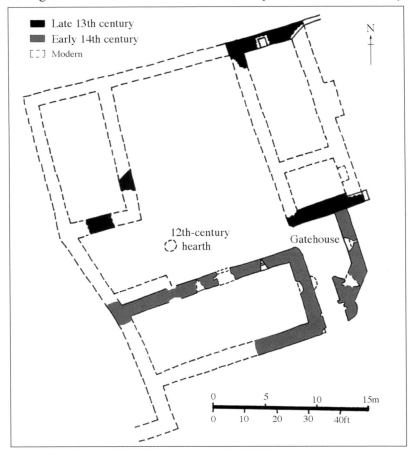

Late 13th century

Early 14th century

Modern

N

12th-century hearth

Gatehouse

0   5   10   15m

0   10   20   30   40ft

of 12th-century artefacts and the presence of a circular enclosure on the 1622 estate map, offer considerable evidence that the first de Barri castle was a ringwork. Unfortunately, nothing survives of this structure.

Now confined to the small plot of land that once formed the inner ward, Barry Castle is a compact ruin dominated by a narrow gatehouse. A section of wall from the 14th-century hall block juts westward from the gatehouse. Both structures were probably built by John de Barri. The ruins of the 13th-century eastern block, a residential wing later transformed into a barn, lead northward from the rear of the gatehouse.

The first stonework at the site was probably the work of Lucas de Barri, who held the manor in the late 13th century. Initial construction focused on the eastern and western ranges. Only a portion of the eastern block – the southern and northern walls – remains standing. Various artefacts, including Roman tiles, an iron chisel and 13th- and 14th-century potsherds, were gathered prior to the destruction of the block's easternmost wall in 1956. The remains of a garderobe were also noted. Most of the western building has been demolished, with the exception of two small chunks of masonry.

John de Barri inherited the castle from his father, Lucas, in about 1300. He soon began an ambitious building effort, which saw the addition of the gatehouse and a southern building, which had a hall on the first floor and a basement below. Historical records offer evidence that a large tower, also added by John de Barri, once stood at the south-western corner of the castle, but the construction of Park Road obliterated this section of the medieval site. During the Second World War, an air raid shelter occupied the spot.

De Barri's gatehouse was a fine structure; however, with walls only just over a metre thick, it probably would have done little to thwart a serious assault. The structure's preservation, such as it is, can be attributed to its use from the mid-17th to the early-18th century as the manorial courthouse. The simple barrel-vaulted passageway was defended by an arrowslit and a portcullis, the grooves of which survive. Inside the gate passage, remnants of the springers that formed the base of an archway indicate that a pair of doors also prevented access. The segment of wall at the rear of the passage still contains an arrowslit, now blocked, and a spiral staircase.

Above the gate passage, the small portcullis room held the windlass mechanism. A piscina and aumbry indicate that the chamber also held the de Barri chapel. At one time, access to this chamber was from the adjoining hall. A single, narrow lancet-headed window faced outward towards the south, as did a larger doorway below. Outside, a drawbridge probably spanned the ditch, long since in-filled.

To the west of the gatehouse, only the interior wall of what was once an impressive hall block still stands. Notable features include traces of a large fireplace, the central doorway with its drawbar holes, and arrowslits facing into the inner courtyard. The hall's eastern wall offered access into the upper level of the gatehouse and also to the wall-walk (or a garderobe?) via a set of stairs in the south-eastern corner. The entire building may have been roofed with Cornish slate and green glazed tiles.

The de Barris held Barry Castle until the mid-14th century, when it passed to Oliver St. John, owner of Fonmon Castle, located not far to the west of Barry. By 1538, when Leland visited the site, it had begun to decay. Later in the 16th century, a tenant, William Wilkyn, transformed the hall block into a public house, apparently keeping prostitutes on the premises. He demolished many of the hall's original features, including the southern wall, removed other ruins, and then built a cottage, 'Castle House', inside. During the 17th century, the site also had a noteworthy garden.

In 1660, the St. Johns sold Barry Castle and manor to Evan Seys of Boverton. In about 1800, the cottage was demolished. During the next 150 years, Barry itself expanded dramatically. Houses began to appear all around the castle site, and portions of the eastern block were incorporated into later construction.

Barry Town Council initially handled the upkeep of Barry Castle, but, with local government reorganisation in the 1990s, the site has become the concern of the Vale of Glamorgan.

Beaupre (Old Beaupre)

Substantial remains of a castle largely built in the
14th to 16th centuries
Location: 2 miles south-east of Cowbridge (ST 009 721)
Access: The external is freely visible from a nearby footpath
and the interior is open from 10am to 4pm

The best way to access the site is to park opposite Howe Mill Farm,
along the minor road that heads south-west from the A48 near St.
Hilary (just east of Cowbridge). A stone stile marks the start of a
footpath that leads directly to the castle, but it takes a brisk uphill
walk of perhaps ¼ mile to actually reach the ruins. When heading
up the hill, be sure to notice the earthworks marking the location of
parkland and fishponds and the narrow, snaking River Thaw, which
probably provided water for the Bassets, once one of Glamorgan's
most important families.

The crumbling ruins of Old Beaupre belie a noteworthy past.
The structure is best labelled a fortified residence, for it was never

intended to offer more than superficial defences for the owners, the Bassets and their descendants, who first occupied the site in 1262. Most of what stands today dates to the 16th century, when the impressive home was given mock battlements and bestowed with the name Beaupre 'Castle'. Portions of the original medieval residence, which was located on a hilltop site of moderate defensive capability, do survive but are well disguised amongst the more lavish Tudor additions. That said, Old Beaupre is one of Glamorgan's finest ruins.

To gain access, walk through a doorway in the gatehouse, which was built in 1586. This features a battlemented roofline, mullioned windows, heraldic emblems, and Richard and Catherine Basset's initials. Richard was the son of William and Catherine Basset, who began the site's transformation into an impressive Elizabethan home.

Inside, the original splendour of the home reveals itself in ornately carved fireplaces and a particularly impressive Tudor porchway, adorned with splendid heraldic emblems and finely carved columns, directly opposite the main gate. The earliest surviving structures, which were possibly part of the medieval castle, stood at this farthest end of the large square courtyard. Among the medieval remains are the tower located immediately left of the porch, and the gatehouse, which is barely visible in the wall adjoining the porch. Most of site's medieval fabric has been incorporated into a private residence at the rear of the site (inaccessible).

Ultimately, the Bassets built two different residences at Beaupre. The first was erected during the early 14th century and still stands in part behind the ornate porch. The second, a mainly 16th-century building, encloses the outer courtyard. Both structures consisted of a square inner courtyard surrounded by domestic ranges and also a main gateway.

In 1376, 'Bewerpere' was first recorded in the ownership of John Basset, who had married an heiress of the de Kardiff family, owners of much of the land in St. Hilary. Old Beaupre remained with the Bassets until the early 18th century, except for a brief time when Elinor Basset, heiress in 1502, was in her minority and her wardship was purchased for Rice Mansel, also in his minority. Even though they married in 1511, Elinor died five years later. Though Mansel remarried, he retained rights to the house until his death in 1559. Rice's daughter, Catherine, married the lawful heir to Beaupre Castle, William Basset, who consequently regained possession of the property. The Mansels and later Bassets gave the site its castellated appearance and lavish ornamentation.

Another Richard Basset supported Charles I during the English Civil War. After the king's defeat, he was forced to pay a hefty fine, which created such a financial strain that he abandoned Beaupre Castle in favour of a more modest home elsewhere. In 1709, Christopher Brewster acquired the site and it became the concern of tenant farmers. The medieval wing was converted into the farmhouse and remains occupied.

Bishopston
(Bishopston Old Castle,
Barland Castle)

Severely eroded ringwork
Location: To the north-east of Bishopston church,
on the Gower (SS 582 900)
Access: A footpath passes somewhat near the site, which itself
is on private property, but the site is difficult to see
due to erosion and the presence of scrub

To approach the site, which is on the southern side of Bishopston Brook, some 0.7km north-east of St. Teilo's Church in the hamlet of Bishopston, park near the quarry on the north side of the B4436 at Bishopston, where the footpath sign clearly points the way. Then, where the pathway splits, take the right-hand branch and continue towards the brook. The site lies on the far side of the brook in the scrub on the right.

The severely eroded ringwork at Bishopston barely survives and the flat-topped platform that encompassed the central area of the ringwork is almost impossible to detect, due to erosion and the presence of horses at the site.

The oval ringwork probably dates to the 12th century, when the Bishops of Llandaff controlled the area (and gave the village its name). Defended on its northern side by the rushing waters of Bishopston Brook and on the remaining sides by a bank and ditch, the ringwork once measured 22 metres by 15 metres. Excavations conducted in 1898 uncovered post-holes and other traces of a timber palisade, an interior stone revetment, and an external ditch, which originally measured 2.5 metres in depth. Artefacts discovered during the dig included a bronze buckle, the soles of leather shoes, and pottery dating to the late 12th or early 13th century.

Bonvilston

Scant earthwork remains
Location: 4 miles east of Cowbridge (ST 071 734)
Access: Site visible from distant footpath, but no direct access

Just to the east of the entrance to the church in Bonvilston, take the footpath that leads off from the opposite side of the road. Go across a field, through a small wood and then follow the footpath down the hedgerow in the next field and then at an angle across it till you pass under the closer set of electricity cables. If you then look left down the line of cables the site of the earthwork is in the valley bottom, just to the left of the cables and this side of some woodland. A tiny stream flows immediately alongside the south-eastern side of the site. The original entrance lies on the eastern side of the castle.

During the 12th and 13th centuries, the Bonville family occupied this area, and the ringwork probably served as the administrative centre of their small manor. In the 13th century, Robert Bonville granted most of Bonvilston to the monks of Margam Abbey, who probably erected the earthworks which are still noticeable to the east of the ringwork.

Briton Ferry

Reputed scant earthwork remains
Location: On a hilltop on the western side of the
River Neath (SS 732 940)
Access: No obvious access

The steep-sided clifftop overlooking the small harbour at Briton Ferry is clearly fortified, for a ditch encircles the end of the promontory. Some historians believe this site coincides with the historical record, which states that Morgan ap Caradog ab Iestyn, the Welsh Lord of Afan, built a castle in the 12th century close to where the River Neath passes Briton Ferry. However, it seems equally reasonable to speculate that the site is an Iron Age promontory fort similar to the one on Warren Hill, on the opposite hilltop. Morgan may or may not have adapted the earlier promontory fort at Briton Ferry for his own purposes while serving as Lord of Afan.

Brynwell
(Beganston or Leckwith)

Negligible extant remains
Location: West of Leckwith village,
itself north-west of Penarth (ST 147 744)
Access: Can be reached by public footpath

Take exit 33 on the M4 and go south on the A4232. Take the second exit, turning right onto the B4267 towards Llandough. At the far end of the village of Leckwith, just before the speed limit derestriction signs, turn right into The Green, and park here. Walk up the lane that leads off The Green from near where you entered it, and bear right when it forks. Stay on the lane and follow the woodland down on the right and shortly after the lane bends left, take the stile in the hedge on the right. Walk across the field heading to the gate at the right of several collapsed farm buildings. The castle site is between the edge of these barns and the derelict farmhouse to the right.

The ringwork at Brynwell Farm once occupied slightly elevated land near the River Ely, which flows about a mile to the east. The earthen embankments were only discovered in the late 20th century; sadly, the northern side had been destroyed, probably when the adjoining rick-yard was built. Originally, the bank and ditch of the ringwork completely encircled an area of about 30 metres. In its heyday, Brynwell probably served as the caput of the Began family, who occupied the site in the 13th century. During the 12th century, the site was the centre of the lordship of Leckwith. The village of the same name is located about ½ mile directly east of Brynwell Farm.

The farmhouse at the site features a trefoil-headed window, certainly of medieval origin, which supports the notion that the castle stood near the spot. The building may in fact incorporate a 14th-century hall that stood in the now-vanished bailey.

Cadoxton Court

Scant remains incorporated into later house
Location: In a residential area on the east of Barry (ST 128 688)
Access: Best seen from the main road below the site in winter
(i.e. when there are no leaves on the trees)

Head into Barry the A4055 from the east. Follow the signs to the Town Centre, and having passed under the railway line, go straight across the roundabout on the far side. Cadoxton Court can be seen almost straight ahead above the road on its right, best identified from the large stone dovecote.

Historical records indicate the existence of a sub-manor at Cadoxton which the Mitdehorguill family held for the price of two knights' service in the 12th century. The site stood at the edge of a steep hillside overlooking a ravine that led toward Barry Sound. The Royal Commission has classified Cadoxton Court as a possible castle and as a medieval house; however, it has long since vanished, except for the circular dovecote, some fragments of medieval masonry now embedded in the later house, and ancillary buildings which may have replaced the medieval house in the 19th century.

Cae-Castell

Some earthwork remains (SN 694047)
Location: 2 miles north-west of Pontardawe
Access: On private ground

Also called Rhyndwychydach or Llechart for its proximity to a farmstead of that name, Cae-Castell is on private property. Take the A474 north-west from Pontardawe. After about 1 mile, just past the end of the built-up area and near a pub, take the minor road left. Once across the river bear left. Keep right at two junctions as the road heads around the hill, and then more sharply right to cross over the hill. The road drops down on the other side and makes a sharp bend once across another river. The grid reference indicates a point on the hillside above the next stretch of road, but nothing is indicated on the recent OS Explorer Map. Stop at Llechart Farm a bit further on up a lane on the right not only to ask permission to visit the site, but also to get specific directions to reach it on foot.

One of Glamorgan's most enigmatic earthwork castles, Cae-Castell sits at the edge of a deep ravine which formed a natural defence on the castle's eastern side. Cae-Castell fails to appear in the historical record, so notions about its origins are pure conjecture. The castle may have been built by a native Welsh family, for not only is the unusual squarish shape atypical for a Norman-built earthwork castle, but its location in Gower Wallicana (the Welshry of Gower) supports the idea that the structure was built by a Welsh lord, probably in the 12th century.

The earthworks at Cae-Castell project outward at an angle at the north-western corner, forming an unusual, mound-like feature that is similar to but not as large as a typical motte. The mound may have supported a small timber tower, possibly an observation point. A sturdy bank and ditch front the north and western sides of the earthwork, and another embankment runs along the southern side.

Caerau

Impressive ringwork remains
Location: On the southern side of Caerau, on the western
fringe of Cardiff, and perched above the A4232 (ST 134 750)
Access: Can be reached by lane and footpath

Take the A48 south-west from Cardiff. Cross the river Ely and
after about another half a mile turn left onto Caerau Lane (also
signposted Western Leisure and Shopping Centre). Take the third
left onto Caerau Road at the end of which you have to make an
awkward left and then right turn so as in effect to carry straight on
along Church Road. Carry on along Church Road right until its end
in some new houses. Then walk along the track which continues
from the end of Church Road and curls up the hill to arrive at the
remains of the 13th-century St. Mary's Church. Walk around the
church ruins to their right to reach the ringwork, itself set within an
enormous Iron Age hillfort.

From a distance, St. Mary's tower seems to be in outstanding
condition. However, the church is a mass of ruined building material, and only the tower and a portion of the 19th-century vestry

40

survive to any extent. The associated cemetery may occupy the site of the castle bailey. Originally a chapel of Llandaff, the church has become a favourite target of vandals. The main entrance into the castle faces St. Mary's.

Wandering inside the elliptical ramparts gives one a real understanding of the effectiveness of the ringwork design, even without its timber defences. The embanked interior has a diameter of about 52 metres at its longest, a ditch still surrounding much of the exterior. A gap in the tree line on the north-eastern side opposite the entrance reveals how the ringwork's builders shrewdly used the inner rampart from the Iron Age hillfort as part of the castle's defence system.

Although almost nothing exists about the ringwork in the historical record, the Royal Commission contends that the castle may have belonged to the Bishops of Llandaff. By the late Middle Ages, however, the Malefant family, tenants of the bishop, held the castle.

Caerau's Iron Age hillfort encompasses virtually the entire triangular spur of land immediately north of the A4232. While hillforts would not normally be included in a book on medieval castles, its excellent condition and the presence of the marvellous ringwork in its north-eastern corner make the ancient site worthy of mention here. One of south-east Wales' largest multivallate hillforts, the three-tiered fort dates to between 700 BC and AD 100, when it probably defended a settlement of some significance.

Caerphilly

Major castle remains
Location: In the centre of Caerphilly (ST 156 971)
Access: In the care of Cadw; a charge is made for admission

Without a doubt, Caerphilly Castle is Glamorgan's, and arguably Wales', greatest castle. The second largest castle in Britain after England's Windsor Castle, Caerphilly is one of medieval Europe's most important fortresses. Accurately restored by the Marquesses of Bute in the 19th and 20th centuries and cautiously reflooded by the Ministry of Works who took over the castle in 1950, Caerphilly stands as a testament not only to the power and wealth of Gilbert de Clare II, Earl of Gloucester and Lord of Glamorgan, but also to the strength of the threat he felt from Llywelyn ap Gruffydd, the last native Prince of Wales.

Even though Caerphilly is a monumental castle of grand proportions, its role in Welsh history was relatively short-lived and came late in the history of British castle-building. Begun in 1268 to showcase de Clare's power and to thwart the increasing threat from the Welsh, Caerphilly Castle fell into decay less than 200 years after its inception. However, during those two centuries the remarkable fortress withstood several sieges, from both Welsh and English forces.

Unlike many castles in Wales, Caerphilly did not replace an earlier Norman fortification. However, 12 centuries earlier the Romans made ample use of the site, constructing a small auxiliary fort on the tree-clad hill, which is visible across the moat from the western bailey. Placed near the confluence of two streams, the Nant y Gledyr and the Nant y Risca, and along the Roman road linking the forts at Cardiff, Gelligaer and Y Gaer, the existence of the fortlet was only proven in 1963. In that year, archaeologists uncovered remnants of its earth and timber defences and identified the rectangular plan typical of 1st-century Roman forts. The Romans apparently abandoned this site in about 150 AD. While some scholars have speculated that the Normans occupied the Roman site prior to the construction of the great stone castle at Caerphilly, no evidence supports this claim. It lay unoccupied until Gilbert de Clare II, Lord of Glamorgan, decided to make it his finest seat. Before construction could begin, however, de Clare embroiled himself in the barons' conflict with King Henry III.

During the first years of Henry III's reign, while he was still in his minority, England's barons reconfirmed the Magna Carta in order the keep the youth in line. However, the king's appointment of 'foreigners', such as Peter des Roches and Peter des Rievaulx, to positions of power within his government, coupled with problems in Wales and France and an ill-timed famine, prompted renewed resentment among the barons. In 1258, a 24-member committee of barons led by Simon de Montfort, Earl of Leicester, and Richard de Clare, Lord of Glamorgan and Earl of Gloucester, produced the Provisions of Oxford, which proposed a 15-man privy council selected by the barons to advise the king and oversee the administration of his government. Henry balked at their demands.

In 1262, Richard de Clare died and the lordship of Glamorgan and the earldom of Gloucester passed to his son, Gilbert II. However, Gilbert did not actually acquire control of his father's vast estates for well over a year, after the begrudging king finally granted de Clare his rightful inheritance. Following in Richard's footsteps, Gilbert had significant concerns about Henry III's handling of his government, and, not surprisingly, he joined Simon de Montfort and the barons in their rebellion.

In January 1264, King Louis IX of France was invited to arbitrate on the dispute and, in the Mise of Amiens, declared the Provisions invalid in favour of Henry III. Enraged, the barons began a series of uprisings around the kingdom, which culminated in May with the Battle of Lewes. Led by de Montfort and de Clare, the rebels resoundingly defeated the king's men and captured not only Henry III and his son, Prince Edward, but also the king's brother, Richard, Duke of Cornwall. While the king was sent to prison in London, the Duke of Cornwall was confined in Kenilworth Castle and Prince Edward in Hereford Castle.

With their royal rivals out of the way, de Montfort, de Clare and Stephen Bersted, Bishop of Chichester, assumed control of the government and established what amounted to England's first parliament, one that included a council of barons and representatives from each borough in the realm. However, because Simon de Montfort became the effective ruler of England, the situation actually undermined the gains the barons had made since Lewes. Many barons felt his reforms were too bold. When the Earl of Leicester chose to ally himself with Gilbert de Clare's nemesis, Llywelyn ap Gruffydd, de Clare had had his fill of de Montfort.

In 1265, de Clare met with Prince Edward, whose escape from Hereford Castle he may have engineered. They gathered an army and marched to Gloucester, which they captured and moved on to Evesham, where Simon de Montfort was killed, butchered and displayed in pieces around England.

The rebellion did not end with de Montfort's death, however. In September, the king seized the estates of the insurgents, who became known as the 'disinherited lords'. Then, in early 1266, the rebel survivors of Evesham gathered at Kenilworth Castle, which they once again garrisoned in the name of Simon de Montfort, and waited for his son, another Simon, to bring reinforcements from France. In the meantime, Gilbert de Clare joined the king's army as they made their way to the rebel fortress. After nine months, the Royalists finally had their victory; yet, their success had nothing to do with their siege engines – rampant disease (probably dysentery) had actually defeated the defenders. Still undaunted, the remaining group of rebels found their way to Ely, where they continued their resistance against the king.

Shortly after the victory at Kenilworth Castle, the Lord of Glamorgan headed back to Wales, where the Welsh had taken the opportunity of his absence to attempt to retake the lands they once held, including Senghennydd. In January, de Clare captured Gruffydd ap Rhys, the hereditary lord of Senghennydd, re-annexed the Welsh lordship and imprisoned Gruffydd, first in Cardiff Castle and then in Ireland. With the Welsh in line, Gilbert headed back to England. Frustrated with the king's reluctance to put an end to the conflict with the barons, he gathered his own army, which included men from Ely, and, in April of 1267, marched to London in support of the disinherited lords, who demanded the return of their hereditary lands. Finally, in September, the king passed the Statute of Marlborough, which allowed the barons to regain their estates.

After the king returned the barons' confiscated lands, de Clare headed back to Wales and began work on his castle. First, he had to settle things with Llywelyn ap Gruffydd, Prince of Wales, whose men destroyed his first effort to build a castle at Caerphilly (see Chapter III). When the Welsh left Glamorgan to fight Edward I farther north in Wales, Gilbert then concentrated on completing his great fortress. By the time it was done, Caerphilly Castle achieved its well-deserved status as Britain's first fully concentric castle, the first of its kind built entirely from scratch (as opposed to being created by additions over time).

Intentionally selecting the low-lying spot, which was surrounded on three sides by high hills, de Clare astutely modelled his new castle on Kenilworth Castle, where he encountered the formidable water defences which influenced the design of his castle at Caerphilly. Ultimately, this 'walls-within-walls' fortress became the archetype for other concentric castles, including those built by Edward I over ten years later to subjugate the Welsh in North and Mid Wales.

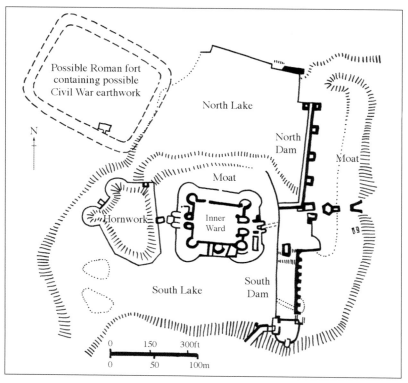

Looking at Caerphilly Castle from a distance, one can easily identify what made the concentric design so valuable to castle-builders: the towers and gatehouses along the outside of the castle were lower than comparable features closer to the centre, where the main business of the castle was conducted. During a siege, the garrison could place themselves on both defensive rings and not worry about hitting their own men when firing down upon the enemy. The dual walls also expanded their field of vision. And, if an enemy managed to breach the outer ring of defences, they would find themselves confined between lower outer and higher inner defensive walls, with the defenders still firing upon them from positions of relative safety overhead.

Caerphilly Castle was not just defended with rings of stonework. Its water defences were an integral part of the concentric plan. They acted as intervening defensive rings, which the enemy had to cross in order to assault and then pass through the progressively taller gateways into the interior. No matter whether attackers used boats or attempted to swim across the lake-like moats, they would find themselves vulnerable to the soldiers inside the castle and unable to properly return their fire.

Today, the town's circular roadworks cover portions of the stronghold, but most of the castle's original medieval perimeter can be walked. The main entrance to the castle opens on the east side, accessed by crossing two bridges, which span the outer moat, and passing through the original outer gatehouse. To either side of the gatehouse, two unusual dams stretch along the entire eastern front of the castle. The northern dam features three massive towers, which are now no longer attached to the walls they were built to support. The ruined twin-towered north gatehouse is accessible from inside the castle and still bars unwanted access at the northernmost end of the dam.

The southern dam lines the bulky southern platform. Built slightly earlier than the northern dam, this chunk of land and stone was used to help create the southern lake. A row of eight vertical buttresses still spans the entire length of the southern dam, which also connects the central platform to the south barbican.

The well-preserved main outer gatehouse was probably erected in about 1220, at the same time as the northern dam. The gate passage was defended by a portcullis and six narrow murder holes, and had guardrooms on either side. The twin polygonal towers were built with Pennant sandstone, their bases supported with angle spurs, and their walls penetrated with cross-oillets and grooves for ropes or chains to raise and lower the drawbridge. Upper floors contained a porter's kitchen with a fireplace and oven and other chambers that gave access to the rooftop. The garrison could access the wall-walk from inside the towers. The stairs into both towers still reach the turret (sometimes known as the Wassail Tower) at the rear of the northern gate tower. Fortunately, the gatehouse was not destroyed during the English Civil War; instead, it was used as a prison.

The construction of the eastern dam created additional platforms. The fairly plain northern platform, mentioned above,

provided access alongside the northern lake, which was added during the third building stage and supposedly supported stables. A watergate and portcullis defended a spillway, which existed beneath the modern walkway.

The southern platform supports an intriguing array of features, including the remains of a medieval mill and replicas of several siege engines, now poised to attack the inner ward. A large rounded area projects outward almost immediately to the east as one heads across the platform. The grassy area (sometimes called the central platform) provided extra space for soldiers to defend that side of the dam. Nearby, on the interior of the southern dam, a short ditch crosses to the water mill, where corn was ground; waters flowing into the ditch powered the wheel. Embedded into the platform, the mill is now extensively ruined, but even so remains a rare example of its kind. Beyond the mill ruins are the reconstructed siege engines. Their medieval counterparts would have been erected on the spot by the attacking army. The models do work, although only during special events, and include a trebuchet, mangonel, perrier, and springald.

At the southernmost end of the platform, a self-contained complex of structures guarded access from the town. A curious ruined cross-wall and downward step separate this area – the south barbican – from the rest of the southern dam. At the very end of the dam, a round-fronted salient, erected during the castle's initial building phase, projects outward. To its west, the twin-towered south gatehouse (sometimes known as Giffard's Tower or the Barbican Gate) still watches over Caerphilly town. Only partially open to the public, the gatehouse has round towers with pyramidal spurs flanking the short gate passage, which was defended with a single portcullis and arrowslits. The deep pits underneath the main passage indicate that the gateway once employed a turning bridge to link with the 'mainland'. John Giffard commanded the king's troops and was involved in the death of Llywelyn ap Gruffydd at Cilmeri in 1282.

On the eastern side of the barbican, the rectangular remains of Felton's Tower overlook the spot where sluice gates once controlled the flow of Nant y Gledyr around the castle. John Felton served as constable during Lord Zouche's onslaught on the castle in the name of Queen Isabella in 1327 (see below). Today, the structure is most notable for its block of latrines (best seen from outside the castle), which emptied into the moat below.

A modern footbridge spans the inner moat to allow access to the inner ward and main complex of castle buildings. During the Middle Ages, the curtain wall surrounding the rectangular inner ward stood much taller than it does now, thus providing a more substantial barrier to an attack. The adjoining two-storey outer eastern gatehouse, with its arrowslits and portcullis, dates from 1277-1283. Though it offered only modest protection from the enemy, once past this gateway, invaders would have found themselves face to face with an enormous, imposing barricade: the great gatehouse and the two formidable round towers planted at either corner of the inner ward. From these three powerful structures, the garrison could effectively defend the interior of the castle.

Immediately to the left on the opposite side of the gatehouse, the sunken shell of an elongated storehouse fills much of the grassy middle ward. Added during the second building phase, the structure now contains only a few features, including two splayed windows.

Beyond the storehouse, the impressive remains of the south-eastern tower lean precariously, as they have for centuries. Still

surviving to its original height, the tower is amazingly intact and features battlements with arrowslits, trefoil-headed lancet windows, and the battered base that originally supported its three storeys. The upper floors once held residential chambers, and a timber hoard probably rimmed the roofline (as indicated by the square holes beneath the crenellations). Contrary to popular lore which claims that Cromwell's troops slighted the tower, archaeologists believe it actually slumped due to subsidence of the underlying ground.

At one time, the middle ward would have surrounded the entire inner ward, but, in about 1280, its southern side was blocked by the addition of the round south tower, inside of which the remains of the kitchen tower and several huge fireplaces still survive. A square kitchen block was added later to supplement the activities in the kitchen tower. Unfortunately, these structures are greatly ruined and presently inaccessible. They were placed at this position to support the activities in the adjoining great hall, which faces into the inner ward. A masonry passageway, known as the 'transverse block', linked the great hall to the kitchen area. Heightened shortly after the south tower was added, the transverse block provided access to the great hall and wall-walk above.

Arguably the finest structure at Caerphilly, the eastern inner gatehouse dominates the interior of the castle. Probably based on the gatehouse at Tonbridge Castle in Kent, which was erected by Gilbert de Clare's father, Richard, the great gatehouse served as the home of the castle's constable. Slighted by Cromwell after the English Civil War, the exterior façade was restored to its original magnificence by the 4th Marquess of Bute in the 1930s. The structure could function as a keep as well as a gatehouse. Its massive round towers and well-defended central passageway guarded the self-sufficient structure.

Begun during the initial building phase in 1268-71, the great gatehouse was the first of its kind in Wales. Two portcullises, heavy wooden doors, murder holes, and arrowslits defended the gate passage; inside the towers, guardrooms filled the lowest level. The placement of guardroom doorways along the passageway and the ability to barricade the gatehouse from both directions made assaulting the structure difficult at best.

The beauty of the great gatehouse can truly be appreciated from the inner ward. Two imposing turrets hold the spiral staircases, which lead to the upper levels and the roof line. Ornate windows pierce the flat western wall. Evidence for timber hoarding and arrowslits survives. Inside, the three first floor chambers fulfilled a military role. The central room housed the portcullis mechanism and gave access to the murder holes. The rooms on either side allowed movement to and from the wall-walk and to conveniently placed garderobes. The uppermost storey probably held the 'constable's hall' mentioned in 14th-century historical documents. The grand chamber would have resembled a lord's great hall; its fine hooded fireplace and huge trefoil windows with side seats (now restored) overlooked the inner ward. A small chamber on the level above the constable's hall at the southern end of the gatehouse may have been used as a chapel or oratory, or perhaps as a strongroom for valuables.

The rectangular design of the inner ward fit well within the moated complex. At each corner, an enormous round tower defended the castle's interior. On the opposite side of the bailey from the great gatehouse, the less complex western gatehouse stood alongside a range of private apartments. To the south, the great hall still fills almost the entire length of the ward; on the opposite side a lengthy curtain wall defended the northern side of the castle. Cadw have added a replica of a covered timber hoard to give visitors a real sense of what soldiers would have experienced when fighting an enemy. At the eastern end of the hoarding, a modern version of a medieval crane demonstrates how troops hauled supplies up to the fighting platform. The exterior of the timber hoarding, the latrine chute outfall, and a postern gate are visible on the opposite side of the wall (which faces the middle ward).

Gilbert de Clare II undoubtedly built his great hall to impress his guests. However, though the interior reflects Gilbert de Clare's original design, now only the southern and end walls date to the 13th century. The structure is mainly the work of Hugh le Despenser and his master mason, Thomas de la Bataile, who raised the level of the floor and rebuilt the northern wall and main doorway. The present building actually contains two areas divided by a cross-wall. An ornate chapel once filled the eastern side of the upper level; underneath, the buttery and pantry were well situated to serve the adjacent hall. The chapel was reached by a set of timber steps leading from the inner ward; the chamber also offered access to an outer room, believed to have been a solar. Unfortunately, much of the chapel's finery, most notably the windows on the south side, has been obscured by modern alterations.

On the eastern side of the great hall, a raised dais once supported the high table and chairs for the lord and his guests. The lord's private apartments stood beyond the opposite, western wall. Behind the southern wall, the kitchen block served the needs of the lord, and another doorway opened into a covered passage which led to the postern gate outside the castle and also to accommodation on the upper level.

Today, heraldic emblems colour the walls, and the remains of the central fireplace hint at the grandeur of Despenser's great hall. Closer investigation reveals skilfully carved stone heads watching over the activities as they did centuries ago. Each corbel features three heads, one of which is crowned and may represent Despenser's king, Edward II. A lavishly bedecked female figure may depict Edward's treacherous wife, Queen Isabella, and one of the bearded faces may be Despenser himself. The corbels also support the modern timber beams which buttress the impressive ceiling restored by the 3rd Marquess of Bute in 1871.

Access to the private apartments, which are now almost completely ruined, is from the inner ward. At one time, the building contained several residential chambers, including a large room with a fine tracery window nearest the hall and another solar. The rooms were well heated with a round-backed fireplace, and the solar once opened to a latrine tower, which no longer survives. A doorway on the lower level originally allowed access to the round south-west tower. The lord's living quarters spanned the upper level. An elongated window overlooking the bailey retains some trefoil and quatrefoil decoration, evidence that someone of status (probably the Lord of Glamorgan and his family) lived inside.

The best preserved of the four corner towers in the inner bailey is the north-west tower, which has a doorway into the ward and a spiral staircase to the upper levels. All four towers probably appeared much the same as this one, except for the placement of the garderobe (the outflow openings are visible from the outside of the castle). The lowest level probably served as a storage area; it was poorly lit and unheated. Upper floors were heated with fireplaces, which survive, and were lit by arrowslits and trefoil-headed windows. A garderobe provided essential comfort on the uppermost level. Restored battlements and a modern roof crown the tower. The walk-walk is still accessible from the first floor.

Like the eastern gatehouses, the two western gatehouses decrease in height from the taller interior structure to the lower outer one; however, both are simpler in design than their eastern counterparts, which served as the castle's main entry points. The inner western gatehouse is in excellent condition and retains much of its original masonry. Only the battlements are reconstructions. The ground floor of the twin-towered structure contained two six-sided guard-rooms, both of which were vaulted and defended through arrowslits and entered from the inner ward. A vaulted gate passage stretched between the two chambers. Murder holes provided defence from above, while two portcullises prevented unwanted access, one at the inner end of the passageway and the second situated mid-passage. Inside the round-fronted towers, newel stairs linked to the upper levels, which held accommodation.

As in the great gatehouse, the upper level of the inner western gatehouse contained one huge chamber with a central fireplace and windows. The windows facing into the castle were ornate and provided plenty of light; those facing outwards were simple and small. Unlike its eastern counterpart, this gatehouse was also fitted with a drawbridge pit; apparently, the medieval bridge was never finished.

Beyond the inner western gatehouse, the grassy middle ward extends around to this side of the castle and provides access to the outer western drawbridge (its two pits survive on either side of the moat) and the outer gatehouse. The two western gatehouses stand at different levels to each other. Possibly built this way to interfere with an assault, the outermost structure now faces directly into the revetment of the western hornwork.

Often called the western island or Y Weringaer ('the people's fort'), some historians speculate that the hornwork, a seemingly open, vulnerable earthwork, may have served as the last place of refuge for local townsfolk during a siege. The irregularly shaped earthen platform is completely encompassed by a low stone revetment wall, which was never completed. What appear to be two rounded stone salients face outward towards the west. Drawbridges linked the hornwork not only to the inner ward, but to the northern side of the castle and also across the moat to near the site of the Roman fort. Remnants of an earthen Civil War redoubt survive on the opposite side of the moat. Constructed in the 1640s by Parliamentarian troops, the redoubt provided a platform from which troops could bombard the castle with cannon fire. It may also have served as a guard post for Cromwell's soldiers who were positioned there to interfere with any reconstruction work.

After executing Llywelyn Bren in 1318 (see Chapter III), Hugh le Despenser became one of the realm's most despised leaders, and, for a brief time, he was exiled from England while Edward II attempted to placate the barons. However, by the end of 1321, the Despensers returned to Britain, having again curried the king's favour, and instigated a move against the barons in support of Edward. At the Battle of Boroughbridge in March 1322, Despenser and his comrades defeated the barons. Afterwards, Despenser continued to consolidate his power base in Wales and the rest of the kingdom, and also made major alterations to his castle at Caerphilly, which included the renovation of the great hall discussed above.

In 1326, however, his fortunes changed and Despenser was forced again to flee into exile, this time with Edward II, when Queen Isabella and her paramour, Roger Mortimer, wrested power from the weak king. For a time, the two men sought refuge in Glamorgan, and, from 29 October to 2 November, sheltered at Caerphilly Castle. Reputedly depositing half the king's treasure at the castle, they then moved on, only to be captured two weeks later near Llantrisant on their way back to Caerphilly. The controversial Lord of Glamorgan was summarily executed on 20 November at Hereford; death by red hot poker awaited the king at Berkeley Castle.

After Despenser and the king left Caerphilly Castle, constable John Felton endured a four-month siege by Isabella's forces, which were under the direction of William, Lord Zouche. As the castle ably withstood the battering, Felton demanded a pardon for himself and Hugh, Despenser's son and heir. In March 1327, he obtained that pardon and surrendered the castle and its provisions, which were said to include a portion of Edward's magnificent treasure. Sadly, the whereabouts of that treasure remain unknown.

Initially, Isabella appointed William, Lord Zouche, as keeper of Glamorgan and custodian of Caerphilly Castle, but she soon granted Glamorgan to Mortimer. In early 1328, Eleanor (de Clare) Despenser regained rights to the lordship of Glamorgan and the castle at Caerphilly. In 1329, Lord Zouche abducted Eleanor, and they married without royal consent. The pair then staged another assault on Caerphilly Castle, ostensibly so that William could claim the rights to the lordship of Glamorgan, which he believed to be his when he married Eleanor. In May of that year, the couple was arrested and Glamorgan again became a royal holding. When Isabella and Mortimer fell from power in 1330, the castle and lordship reverted to Eleanor de Clare and her husband.

Imprisoned since 1327 when Caerphilly first fell to Lord Zouche, Eleanor's son, Hugh, finally gained his freedom in 1331. Acquiring Glamorgan six years later, Lord Despenser held the lordship until his death in 1349. At the inquisition post mortem, Caerphilly Castle was declared to have virtually no value, being only worth reprises plus the profits that could be made from selling the fish in the lakes.

After Hugh Despenser's death, Caerphilly Castle passed to Edward Despenser, then to Edward's widow, Elizabeth, and then to their son, Thomas Despenser. When Thomas was executed for treason in 1400 (having sought to restore Richard II to the throne in place of the usurper, Henry IV), his widow, Constance, received Glamorgan, but, the castle remained with Elizabeth Despenser. Caerphilly Castle remained unscathed during the Glyndwr rising in the early 1400s.

In 1416, the lordship of Glamorgan passed to Isabel, the Despenser heiress, whose husbands each gained rights to Caerphilly Castle through marriage. Isabel's first husband, Richard Beauchamp, Earl of Worcester, died in 1422; she remarried another Richard Beauchamp, this time the Earl of Warwick, the following year. From 1428-1429, the earl made the last substantial repairs to the castle, improving Felton's Tower and building a new prison inside the outer gatehouse. After Beauchamp died in 1439, the Earls of Warwick increasingly neglected Caerphilly in favour of their more lavish residences elsewhere. By the time Jasper Tudor acquired the lordship in 1486, Caerphilly Castle had declined to the point that it was no longer of enough importance to be extensively repaired.

Later owners included Henry Somerset, tenant for life (1496-1526); William Herbert, Earl of Pembroke (1551-70); and Henry Herbert, Earl of Pembroke (1570-1601), who leased the castle to Thomas Lewis in 1593. Lewis then quarried the stronghold for its masonry, which he used for his own residence, Y Fan (The Van).

Photographs of Caerphilly Castle taken by Francis Frith in 1871 and 1874 reveal a grand castle in a severe state of decay. Ivy-covered, crumbling walls dominated the site, and the water defences were dry and grass-filled. The first Marquess of Bute acquired Caerphilly Castle by right of marriage to the heiress of the Earls of Pembroke and began consolidating the ruins. However, he left it to his descendants to undertake the major alterations that prevented the castle from further deteriorating. It was not until the 3rd Marquess inherited the site in the 1870s that a concerted effort was made to restore the structure to its original splendour.

Candleston

Roofless ruins of a fortified residence
Location: On the edge of the dunes 3 miles the south-west
of Bridgend (SS 872 773)
Access: Sits just above a public car park and can be seen
at any time

From the A48 to the south-west of Bridgend take one of the minor roads heading south signposted to Merthyr Mawr. Continue through the village, passing the church on your right, and continue along the road which ends in a car park by the dunes. Candleston Castle sits above the car park, on the right as you enter it.

Candleston Castle is one of four structures in Glamorgan characterised as a 'tower house', a significantly fortified residence built to impede brief assaults rather than to withstand prolonged sieges. Now considerably ruined, the site initially consisted of a D-shaped perimeter wall which enclosed the outer end of a promontory overlooking Merthyr Mawr warren and its encroaching sands. Given the proliferation of ringworks in the region and the layout of Candleston Castle, it is possible that the stronghold was built on the site of a ringwork; however, nothing survives to verify this assumption.

Part of the fee of Merthyr Mawr and owned by the St. Quintins in the late 12th century, the manor was leased to the de Cantelupe family who gave the building its name. During the 13th and 14th centuries, the de Cantelupes played key roles in the politics of Glamorgan, but it is unclear which heir actually constructed the masonry castle: Robert de Cantelupe III, who died in 1320; John de Cantelupe, reputedly an abbot at Margam Abbey; or Nicholas de Cantelupe, who probably held the manor from about 1330 to 1366.

Most of what survives is fairly unremarkable, except for the exquisite fireplace on the south side of the hall and the unusual tower house. Perhaps reflecting the location of the original ring-work, a low curtain wall curves around the western and southern sides of the outer ward (also known as a barmkin). Obscured by bracken and trees and greatly decayed, the wall was built with Carboniferous limestone rubble to buttress the hillside, which sloped steeply and was valued for its natural defences. The original gateway would have stood approximately where visitors now walk onto the grounds.

Candleston Castle's domestic range is dominated by the hall, centrally located service buildings and two rooms beyond. A huge basement fireplace indicates the site of a kitchen added in the 15th century when the hall was heightened (the bake oven dates to the 1800s). Built with greenish sandstone, the ornate chimneypiece on the hall's elaborate first-floor fireplace is one of the highlights of the site. Residents stopped using the two northernmost chambers in about 1800 after blocking them up during the castle's final construction phase. Today, only portions of the western walls survive.

Still rising to its original height of eight metres, the adjoining two-storey tower house was constructed in the 14th century, just after the hall block was completed. A doorway alongside the great fireplace actually allowed the de Cantelupes to withdraw from the hall into the solar, which occupied the first floor of the tower house. Even though the solar is a shell, it does retain a fireplace and a well-preserved garderobe. Traces of wall-walk survive at the second storey level. At ground level, a vaulted undercroft remains in fine condition. A set of stairs leads into the dark basement, where wine and other items were once stored.

After Nicholas de Cantelupe died in 1366, ownership of the manor and castle of Candleston passed to Sir William Horton by right of marriage to Joan de Cantelupe, daughter of Richard de Cantelupe III. In 1468, their daughter, Janet, passed the castle by right of marriage to her husband, Richard Cradock.

Candleston Castle remained a Cradock possession for about another 50 years. It then passed to the Earls of Pembroke when Margaret, Sir Matthew Cradock's heiress, wed Sir Richard Herbert. The Herberts mainly contributed the blocky structure that still projects into the courtyard next to the hall. Today, only the exterior of this so-called 'west wing' survives in decent condition; the interior is a shell.

In 1617, Sir William Doddington acquired Candleston Castle by marriage to the Herbert heiress. Sir William's granddaughter, in turn, passed the castle and associated manor to her husband, Robert Greville, 4th Baron Brooke of Warwick. The Grevilles continued to own and occupy the site until the 18th century, when they sold it to the Franklens.

In about 1800, during the final phase of construction, portions of the curtain wall were stabilised and the stableblock to the north of the tower house was added. Today, the empty rectangular building is filled with vegetation and rubble. In 1830, John Nicholl purchased Candleston Castle from Richard Franklen and it became an integral part of the Merthyr Mawr estate. It remains so to this day. The castle was finally abandoned in the 19th century, after use as a farmhouse.

When they built Candleston Castle, the de Cantelupes probably did not recognise the dangers posed by the movement of the sand dunes, which the low curtain wall now barely contains. Interestingly, the base of what was probably a medieval windmill was revealed when the sands shifted in 1823. The structure may pinpoint the location of a settlement once associated with the castle.

Cardiff

Norman motte and bailey castle and later extended castle much
adapted by the Marquess of Bute
Location: In the centre of Cardiff (ST 181 766)
Access: Open most days throughout the year for a fee

Cardiff Castle's mundane exterior belies the magnificence that
awaits the visitor inside the curtain wall, grandeur embellished by
the Marquesses of Bute during the 19th century but begun much
earlier. At one corner, the imposing Clock Tower stands as a monument to the Bute influence in South Wales, but the true glory of
the medieval castle — the great motte and shell keep — occupies
the interior. In many ways, they are its most awe-inspiring treas-
ures. Visitors must pay for a guided tour of the Bute/Burges interiors, which startle the senses with their giltwork, sweeping vaults,
brilliant colours, and mythical creatures. The lavish decor offers
insight into the mindset and social order of the 19th century, when
the Butes made their fortunes and transformed Cardiff into a leader

of the industrial world. The castle itself was placed in the care of the local authority in 1947.

The city's Welsh name, Caerdydd, reflects its Roman origins, 'caer' meaning 'fort' in Latin. The layout of the castle reflects the rectangular plan of the last of four Roman forts that occupied the spot. Remnants of Roman masonry survive in the medieval curtain wall itself. The Romans chose this spot because of its strategic value: not only did it lie along a major east/west Roman road across Wales, but its location near Cardiff Bay and at a fording point along the River Taff also gave it access to the sea and a major communications route.

The first fort at the site was occupied from about 55 to 90 AD, and covered about 12 hectares. The second was smaller and operated during the very late 1st century. The third fort, built a century later, occupied much the same site but also included a more elaborate gateway and facilities for iron-smelting. The fourth and final Roman-era fort, begun between 276 and 285 AD, was active for about a century.

Only discovered in 1889, the entire circuit of the 4th-century Roman walling has been excavated by archaeologists. The wall originally featured several five-sided towers, traces of which survive in some places. Parts of the medieval curtain wall were built on top of their Roman predecessors, which together actually formed a nine-sided polygonal shape and not a perfect rectangle as was typical of Roman forts in Britain. Fragments are still visible in the later medieval walls as reddish courses outlining the lowest levels. Of particular significance are the ruins of the north gateway, the footings of which survive, flanked by two towers, at the rear of the Norman motte (the present north gateway was extensively reconstructed by the Marquess of Bute in the 19th century).

One of the finest examples of its kind, the Norman motte and bailey castle at Cardiff dominates the inner ward. Constructed from glacial boulders and gravel, the great mound is the largest in Wales, measuring 33 metres in diameter and rising 10.67 metres. The deep ditch enclosing the motte is still water-filled on the northern and eastern sides. The impressive polygonal shell keep replaced the original unreliable, flammable timber tower that stood atop the motte. The associated bailey incorporated remnants of the Roman fort, the walls of which the Normans either covered with earthen embankments or rebuilt to form the outer boundary of the inner ward. Timber palisades would have once topped the earthworks enclosing the bailey.

In 1081, William the Conqueror built the first Norman castle at Cardiff; however, it was not until Robert Fitzhamon became Lord of Glamorgan in about 1093 that Cardiff became the administrative centre (the caput) of the lordship. Then, Fitzhamon strengthened the castle's defences and erected several other structures to create a fairly formidable stronghold. During Robert Fitzhamon's tenure as Lord of Glamorgan, Cardiff Castle served a variety of purposes. It was the 'comitatus' (county court), the exchequer, the chancery, and the prison, and probably contained a mint as well. It also contained houses ('domi') of the knights of the shire, who were obligated to the Lord of Glamorgan to pay their military obligation by serving as castle guard (castle-ward) and attending the monthly court. Today, only the foundations of some of these houses survive underneath the ground near the motte.

After Robert Fitzhamon died in 1107, Robert FitzRoy, Earl of Gloucester, succeeded as Lord of Glamorgan. He became the owner of Cardiff Castle as a result of his marriage to Fitzhamon's daughter and heiress, Mabel, which probably occurred in 1113. It was Earl Robert who added the impressive shell keep, most likely in response to the Welsh rebellion of 1136. During this time, Robert, Duke of Normandy, who was both William the Conqueror's eldest son and FitzRoy's uncle, was imprisoned at the castle. Even though he was the rightful heir to the English throne, Robert had actually received the duchy of Normandy as his legacy, whereas his younger brother, William (Rufus), was crowned as England's new king upon their father's death in 1087. However, several Norman lords took the opportunity to support a rebellion against William II, ostensibly to support their stand that Robert (also known as Robert Curthose and Robert, the 2nd Duke of Normandy) was the lawful king. Some five years of discord ensued, but Rufus remained king.

In 1096, Duke Robert mortgaged Normandy to Rufus and headed off to the First Crusade. During Robert's absence, William was killed while out hunting in the New Forest in 1100 and his youngest brother, Henry, became King of England. Duke Robert finally decided to claim the English throne as his own, and in 1106 provoked a battle with his brother, Henry I, at Tinchebray, in Normandy. After his defeat by the English army, Robert was sent first to England and then onward to Cardiff Castle, where he lived in relative comfort until his death 28 years later.

In 1158, Cardiff Castle successfully withstood an assault by Ifor ap Meurig (Ifor Bach), Lord of Senghennydd. The inhabitants, William, Earl of Gloucester, his wife, and their baby son, were, however, abducted and, possibly, held captive in nearby Castell Coch until ransom demands were met.

Useful both as the lord's residence and as a refuge in times of siege, the 12-sided shell keep retains its Norman character. Today, it no longer shields the timber buildings that once stood against the interior walls, but a large fireplace and corbels mark their original location. A drawbridge, portcullis, guardroom, the vital well, a wall-walk, and a series of restored battlements complete the Norman stronghold.

Beginning in the 13th century, the de Clares made significant alternations to the keep and the main gateway, which they strengthened in case of a Welsh rebellion. A steeply-angled set of stairs offers access to the summit of the motte, where the imposing gatetower, added by the de Clares before the early 14th century, opens into the shell keep. The seven-sided gatetower rises three storeys and was defended by a series of arrowslits and drawbars, which barricaded timber doors. The first-floor held the hall and an essential garderobe; the second storey still contains well-preserved Tudor window frames.

For some four hundred years, the stairs into the keep were defended by a substantial forebuilding, also built by the de Clares. Now only consisting of foundations, the forebuilding had two smaller gatehouses at each end and projected outward beyond the gatetower to cover the staircase. It was demolished in the 18th century.

In addition to the forebuilding, the de Clares constructed the Black Tower and a south gate to Cardiff Castle to fortify the main gateway. Ruinous in the 19th century, the restored Black Tower dominates the entrance into the inner ward just right of the gateway. Essentially two towers in one, the Black Tower consists of a larger three-storey tower on the south and a smaller one which projects westward. It features finely dressed windows, fireplaces and a stair turret. The cesspit into which three latrine chutes once dumped survives in the basement of the smaller annex.

The Black Tower probably housed the castle prison, and also held living quarters on the upper floors for the gatekeeper or constable. Notable prisoners included Sir William Fleminge, who was executed immediately outside the prison door, and also two priests, Father Philip Evans and Father John Lloyd, who were gaoled together. For a year during the reign of Queen Mary Tudor, Rawlins White was imprisoned at Cardiff Castle, before being burned at the stake. Today, the tower contains the Museum of the Welsh Regiment.

Cardiff Castle was a major administrative centre from 1217-1314, when the de Clares served as Lords of Glamorgan. The replacement of custodian Hubert de Burgh (the king's justiciar) with Peter des Riveaulx in 1232 contributed to the barons' rebellion against Henry III, which Richard Marshal, Earl of Pembroke, led the following year. By 1232, Henry III had incurred the anger of his Norman barons in England for appointing too many 'foreigners' — family and associates from France — to positions of power. One of these men was the Poitevin Peter des Roches, Bishop of Winchester, who became Henry's justiciar in place of de Burgh (he had also served as Regent after the death of William Marshal in 1219 and was King John's justiciar even earlier). Being des Roches' nephew and because his most important roles were as the king's keeper of the wardrobe, the treasurer of his household and the keeper of the privy seal, Peter des Rievaulx was equally unpopular with the barons. Joined by the Welsh, Marshal seized Cardiff Castle and others in Glamorgan and forced the removal of des Riveaulx.

The last de Clare Lord of Glamorgan was Gilbert III, who died at Bannockburn in 1314. After his death, Cardiff Castle reverted to royal custody. It was managed first by Bartholomew de Badlesmere, then by Payn de Turberville, Lord of Coity, and then by John

Giffard, who held the castle until it was formally granted to Hugh le Despenser, the younger, in 1317.

Despite the barons' rebellion against Despenser in 1321 and the flight of Edward II and Despenser, which began at Cardiff Castle in 1326, the castle survived unscathed. In 1404, however, the castle and town fell to Owain Glyndwr and stayed in his hands till 1406. In 1416, Cardiff Castle passed to Isabel, the Despenser heiress. Her husband, Richard Beauchamp, Earl of Worcester, became the owner and Lord of Glamorgan by right of marriage.

In 1423, Isabel Despenser married yet another Richard Beauchamp, Earl of Warwick, who initiated a major building programme at Cardiff Castle, which took it into the modern era of comfort and style. The fine block of buildings rimming the western side of the curtain wall has come to be called the western apartments, for obvious reasons. Beauchamp's building now comprises the central core of this range. Featuring the octagonal tower now known as the Beauchamp Tower, which guarded the medieval town's western gateway, the structure has been greatly modified over the centuries. It is now adorned with an elaborate spire added by the Marquess of Bute in the 19th century.

The three-storey apartment block also contained the hall, two other chambers, a butler's room, and the porter's room. It was fronted by four vaulted turrets, which still project into.the inner ward. Two of the turrets contained staircases. Battlements constructed along the roofline were mainly for decorative effect. Over time, the western apartments were extended and modified, and the hall was eventually divided into a first-floor library and an upper level banqueting hall. On the southern end of the apartment range is the square Herbert Tower, built by Henry Herbert, Earl of Pembroke, who held the castle from 1570 to 1601.

Earl Henry made extensive repairs to Cardiff Castle, which had been neglected by previous owners, improving the kitchen block, exchequer, shire hall, and residential chambers. He added new chimneys, fireplaces, and staircases and made repairs to the Black Tower and the south gate. Herbert also redecorated the interiors of the western apartments, turning them into showcases fit for royalty.

During the English Civil War, Cardiff served as a Royalist stronghold and was governed by a series of custodians. Charles I used the castle in 1645 to gather supporters for his final campaign, but Parliamentarian troops quickly captured it. The following year, Royalist troops besieged but did not take the castle. After Cromwell's final victory against the king, he ordered Cardiff Castle to be slighted in 1649.

In 1766, Charlotte, heiress to the Herbert estates, married John, Viscount Mountstuart, the 3rd Earl (and 1st Marquess) of Bute. The Butes initiated the dramatic changes for which the castle is acclaimed today and ultimately transformed it not only into a modern residence but also into an exotic fantasy fortress. Besides making essential repairs to and restoring various structures, including the Roman wall, the Black Tower, and lengths of the Norman curtain wall, the 3rd Marquess of Bute, John Patrick Crichton Stuart, initiated construction of the fanciful Clock Tower, which is often perceived as the embodiment of the medieval castle, but is actually not medieval at all.

Prior to the recent construction of the new visitor centre, archaeologists discovered more medieval-era finds from the site, including remnants of a kiln, pottery, decorated window glass, iron nails, and part of a scabbard.

Castell Bolan
(Cwm Clais)

A motte
Location: On a hillside promontory looking inland,
north-west of Port Talbot (SS 768 920)
Access: On private land

The motte stands about 25 feet high and is on a hillside spur, partly hidden by trees. The oval mound is surrounded on three sides by natural escarpment, with a ditch cut on the southern side to separate it from the hillside.

Castell Bolan has been the subject of controversy for some time, thanks to its quirky design and the lack of historical evidence to identify its builder. Speculation exists that the earthwork castle may have been built by the Welsh Lord of Afan, perhaps Morgan Gam, in the 12th century. A dip near the centre of the mound may indicate origins as a ringwork; however, CARN: the database of the Royal Commission on Ancient and Historical Monuments in Wales classifies the site as a small motte.

The hollowed area at the south-eastern corner of the site may contain the remains of a collapsed stone-built tower. At some time during the castle's history, a shelf-like structure was cut about midway down the northern slope of the mound. Some historians speculate that the shelf may have held a tower, but no physical evidence has been identified to support this notion. The castle site has not been excavated.

Castell Coch

A medieval castle much whimsified by the Marquess of Bute
Location: Near the junction of the A470 and M4
to the north of Cardiff (ST 131 826)
Access: In the care of Cadw and open throughout the year
for a fee

Take the A470 north from the M4 motorway at junction 32 to the Tongwynlais exit, which is located about five miles from Cardiff. Follow the signs to the castle.

At Castell Coch, the 3rd Marquess of Bute, John Patrick Crichton Stuart, used his fortune and his friendship with William Burges, one of the most imaginative and skilled architects of his era, to recreate what is arguably Glamorganshire's most whimsical castle. However, despite being heavily restored, the modern castle does incorporate portions of the medieval stronghold.

More than likely the Normans erected the first castle at Tongwynglais in the late 11th century as one of a series of mottes probably built to defend the then unfortified settlement at Cardiff (prior to the construction of that castle). Today, the motte is heavily disguised underneath 13th-century grey limestone and red sandstone (hence, its name, 'Castell Coch', which translates as the 'red castle') and the reconstruction work done in the late 19th century.

Gilbert de Clare II, Lord of Glamorgan, built the masonry castle in two separate phases. In 1268, de Clare encased the northern and western sides of the motte with stone. He then erected a thin curtain wall around the summit of the castle, creating what was in essence a large shell keep. He also added a spurred drum tower, now known as the kitchen tower, to the south-western end of the wall. Immediately to the east of the kitchen tower, de Clare constructed a rectangular hall block which linked to a gatehouse and the remainder of the shell wall. Once construction was complete, de Clare built two more enormous round towers: the well tower, on the north-eastern side of the gateway, and the so-called keep tower on the south-east, which also had spurred buttressing. The only medieval reference to the castle reveals that Joan of Acre, Gilbert de Clare II's widow, held Castell Coch, then called 'Castrum Rubeum', until her death in 1307.

During the 1870s, the 3rd Marquess of Bute began his massive building project at Castell Coch. In order to make a thorough survey of the site, William Burges first completely cleared the ruins. Excavations revealed traces of the medieval gatehouse among the remains, but so little survived that Burges rebuilt the entire structure. He also located the basement level of the kitchen tower, which featured two arrowslits and vaulting, and the original layout of the keep tower, which had fragments of ribbed vaulting, two arrowslits, and a latrine chute that linked the keep to the adjoining hall block. Inside the third tower, Burges discovered the well, which contained pieces of charred timber. Noting the presence of small ventilation shafts, he speculated that the well tower was used as a medieval prison. The clearance work exposed evidence of undermining and a destructive fire, which may have occurred when the Welsh destroyed Castell Coch in 1314.

Despite its gaily coloured trim, the stark simplicity of the inner ward belies the gaudy flamboyance of the interior chambers. Burges unfortunately died in 1881, before the interiors could be completed, so William Frame continued the work. Using sketches created by Burges, Frame finally finished the interiors in 1891.

The cobbled interior courtyard stretches just 17 metres across and is surprisingly compact. From here, it is easy to envisage how the medieval shell keep supported vital living spaces, such as the great hall, kitchen, living quarters, and servants' quarters. Doorways from the three main towers opened into the courtyard and allowed movement between the buildings. The timber platform that surrounds much of the inner ward provided access to first-floor chambers.

A set of covered stairs leads from the courtyard into the great banqueting hall, the first of the 'Castellan Rooms'. This enormous chamber spans the entire length of the curtain wall between the keep and kitchen towers. Supported by two long timber beams, the hall's impressive ceiling is decorated with stencilled wooden panels. Adorning wall tops, fine murals accentuated with painted arcading and portraits display the violent deaths of several Christian martyrs. The ornate fireplace hood is crowned by a figure of St. Lucius, who perpetually watches over the rather dull, utilitarian furniture.

Using G.T. Clark's survey as a guide, Burges also embarked on a grand plan to recreate the castle's kitchen at the western end of the banqueting hall. Equipped with three fireplaces, the circular chamber now features Victorian furniture; the two upper floors remain unfurnished.

Below the banqueting hall, the servants' quarters occupy the site of the original medieval hall, of which only the vaulted lower level survived into the late 19th century.

Burges and Bute unleashed their imaginations inside the keep tower, where dazzling displays of romantic revivalism represent the height of Victorian fantasy. The lower levels contain the drawing room, an octagonal chamber crowned with a two-storey high ribbed dome and embellished with brilliant colours and brightly gilded vaulting. Floral designs and a variety of birds, mice, lizards, monkeys, foxes, caterpillars, and butterflies adorn the walls and ceiling. Stars light up the painted skies inside the dome, while scenes from Aesop's fables and Greek mythology flourish in bold relief. The exotic room is filled with symbols of life and death, themes said to have been particularly meaningful to the Marquess of Bute.

Lady Bute's bedroom was located on the upper floor of the keep tower. As below, gay colours emboldened with gilding and mirrors illuminate the double-domed chamber. Painted birds, monkeys, squirrels, and mythological creatures grace the walls, and an elaborate arcade encircles the room with Moorish inspiration. A small garderobe was discreetly located within the thickness of the walling. The startlingly simplistic furniture supposedly harkens back to medieval times. In the end, Lady Bute spent little time at Castell Coch, and her children only visited when they needed to be quarantined.

Adjacent to the keep tower, the gatehouse contains Lord Bute's bedroom and the windlass room, which still houses the heavy mechanisms for moving the turning bridge and portcullis. Initially, Bute had placed his bedroom on the level directly over the gate passage, but the commotion created by the drawbridge and portcullis was so disturbing that he moved the winding mechanism into the lower room and hauled his personal belongings up to the second storey.

The lord's fireplace is simply decorated, with a skilfully carved frieze that runs around the chimneypiece. As in his wife's chamber, Bute also installed what appears to be very functional furniture, and apparently made use of a rather uncomfortable porcelain hip-bath. In 2001, Cadw restored Lord Bute's bed and reinstalled it in the room. In storage since 1940, caretakers did not recognise the bed because it had been disassembled and parts stored in disparate places at the castle.

Even though Castell Coch was finished in 1891, Lord Bute rarely stayed at this Welsh residence. Stables, the chapel, and administrative offices were planned but never built. Bute did attempt a small vineyard on the slopes beneath the castle and reputedly produced wine good enough for use in religious services.

John Patrick Crichton Stuart, the 3rd Marquess of Bute, died in 1900, leaving Castell Coch to his descendants, who placed the building in the care of the Department of the Environment in 1940.

Castell Moel
(Liege Castle)

A hilltop moated site with some earthwork remains
Location: 3 miles east of Cowbridge (ST 054 734)
Access: Footpath passes around the northern edge of the
earthworks

Head towards Cowbridge from Bonvilston along the A48, and take the second road left, turning left again at the next junction. You want to park on the left just after the next road junction at which a roads turns off to the right for Llantrithyd. Walk on up the hill for about a 100 yards to the lane on the left where there is a chapel that has been converted into a house. A footpath leads left here aiming just to the left of the summit of the hill and you will quickly come to the earthworks, which should be just on your right.

Situated atop a small Iron Age hillfort, the ramparts of which survive on the western end of the site, the rectangular moated site is best seen on the northern side. Remnants of the ditch line the northern and eastern sides, where a sunken area may indicate the location of the manor house that reputedly stood here. The site may date to the 13th century.

Cil Ifor

Substantial earthwork remains
Location: On the hillside above and to the east of Llanrhidian on the Gower (SS 505 923)
Access: Clearly visible from nearby roads

There is no public footpath onto the site, but it is clearly visible from nearby roads, notably the minor road to its south.

Many Iron Age hillforts were modified during the Middle Ages to accommodate earth and timber castles. On the Gower Peninsula, the south-eastern corner of lanky Cil Ifor hillfort was apparently reshaped into a small but useful ringwork. Although no historical records document the existence of a castle at Cil Ifor, scholars believe it was probably erected by the de Turbervilles before the middle of the 12th century. Today, a single bank swings around the northern and eastern sides of the oval castle, and, on the southern and eastern sides, an embankment from the hillfort forms the rest of the ringwork.

Cil Ifor hillfort is the largest of its kind on the Gower. A multivallate site, the hillfort was defended by a series of three embankments and ditches. Archaeologists have determined that at least three hut sites stood on the summit, at the north-western end of the fort; the entrance was at the south-west.

Coed-y-Cwm

Some earthwork remains
Location: Half a mile south-west of St. Nicholas, itself
on the A48 between Cowbridge and Cardiff (ST 083 737)
Access: No public access

Historical documents suggest that Coed-y-Cwm was probably the caput of the Mitdehorguill family. Nothing else is known about its history. Perched at the edge of a ravine, the tree-clad site is enclosed by a well preserved ditch. A counterscarp bank defends the north-western side of the castle. Excavations in the 1960s revealed the remains of two stone-and-metal piers, which flanked either side of the entranceway. Archaeologists also discovered stone slabs atop the embankment and 12th-century potsherds.

Coity

Substantial stone remains
Location: In the centre of Coity, 2 miles north-east
of Bridgend (SS 923 816)
Access: In the care of Cadw, and open daily 9.30 to 4

Take the A4061 south at exit 36 of the M4 motorway. After half a mile turn left at a roundabout to Coity. Follow the road into the village and immediately after the post office on your left, turn left on to Heol Spencer, and then right onto the track quickly reached to find the main entrance where you can park.

Variously called 'Coytiff', 'Cortiff', 'Coitiff', 'Coitif', 'Coityf', and 'Coety', Coity Castle served as the caput of the lordship of the same name. The stronghold consisted of two baileys – one round, the other rectangular – and was surrounded by a deep, possibly water-filled, ditch, built to overlook the Vale of Glamorgan.

Coity's earliest history is tied to its location on the western fringes of the lordship of Glamorgan, which was defended as early as the late 11th century by earth and timber castles at Ogmore and Newcastle Bridgend as well as at Coity. Not surprisingly, the three ringwork castles have strong architectural affinities; indeed, in many ways, Coity and Ogmore are particularly similar, despite having different builders. The first written record of a castle at Coity does not appear until 1126, when Payn de Turberville controlled the lordship of Coity. Payn ('the Demon', or 'Y-Cythraul' in Welsh) probably established a castle at Coity shortly after Robert Fitzhamon gained the lordship of Glamorgan.

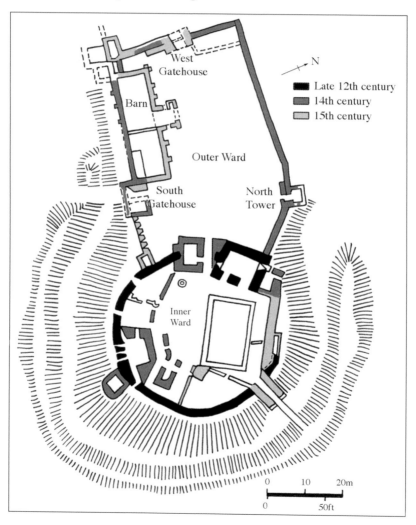

Speculation persists about who actually built the first castle at Coity. Some claim that its builder was the Welshman, Morgan Gam, Lord of Afan, but most support the claim that the Normans erected the original ringwork. Stories suggest that Payn de Turberville did not acquire his lordship at Coity by 'normal' means. Apparently, Robert Fitzhamon forced de Turberville to find his own lordship rather than granting him a particular territory to govern, as he done for so many of his loyal supporters. Venturing into the lordship of Coity, which was then held by the Welsh, Payn discussed its acquisition with Morgan Gam, the Welsh leader. Morgan reputedly agreed to Payn's demand, but had one condition: either the Norman had to fight the Welshman for the lordship or he had to marry Sybil, Morgan's daughter. Payn symbolically took Morgan's proffered sword in his left hand and clutched Sybil with his right. They married, and Sir Payn de Turberville became Lord of Coity. To compound the lack of normalcy in the creation of the lordship, rather than providing soldiers for military service, as was required of most castle owners, the de Turbervilles held the lordship by 'serjeanty of hunting'; their feudal obligation was to provide a place for the Lords of Glamorgan and others to hunt game.

During their three centuries in Glamorgan, the de Turbervilles established a significant power base at Coity and took the castle through its most notable building periods. The earliest record of a castle dates to between 1207 and 1214, when the '*castellum suum de Coitif*' was mentioned in reference to straying livestock from Margam Abbey. The castle then belonged to Gilbert de Turberville II, who, like his ancestor, had married a Welsh heiress from the lordship of Afan. With that marriage, de Turberville extended his family's possessions to include Landimore, in the lordship of Gower, and Newcastle Bridgend.

An impressive sight, Payn de Turberville's ringwork castle is best viewed from the exterior at the north-eastern side which faces St. Mary's Church. The extensive remains include massive earthworks (which are topped by later stone walls), the deep dry ditch, and the well preserved gatehouse. The adjoining bailey contained residential quarters and structures required to administer the caput for the lordship of Coity.

Of the original castle, substantial earthworks still enclose the inner ward; however, the later rectangular western ward probably supplanted the ringwork's outer bailey. At one time, a ditch surrounded the entire inner bailey, which had a 40-metre diameter. Access from the outer bailey would have been via a wooden bridge. During later building periods, the boundary between the two baileys was in-filled and two towers were constructed at the junction. One tower faced northwards and is now greatly ruined. The second tower faced south and was converted into a gateway, which still admits visitors to the outer earthworks.

The curtain wall survives in excellent condition, except for the facet overlooking the north, which Owain Glyndwr's men destroyed in 1404-1405. (It was later repaired.) Otherwise, the original masonry walls, built of rubble and adorned with fine Sutton stone, still enclose the entire inner bailey. Measuring 1.8 metres thick, the eastern walling is the best preserved; portions of the wall-walk can still be identified.

Payn de Turberville II's great keep, begun in the late 12th century, is now heavily damaged. Of the four levels, only portions of its north and western walling and the central piers still stand to any extent. The piers retain their medieval springers and rise from ground floor to the first storey. The ribbed vaulting dates to the 14th century, when the middle gatehouse and northern annexe were added to either side of the keep. Entry into the rectangular structure would have occurred at first-floor level via a movable ladder. The great hall probably occupied this level; well preserved pieces of floor paving survive. Above, residential chambers once served the private needs of the lord and his family.

During the 14th century, the de Turbervilles (probably Payn III and his son, Gilbert IV) initiated an intensive building programme, which included the construction of a simple gateway and a curtain wall with three square towers around the outer bailey. North of the keep, the new three-storey rectangular annexe provided additional accommodation; a doorway at first-floor level probably linked the two structures.

Like the keep, the topmost level of the annexe dates to the 16th century, when Thomas Gamage probably occupied the castle. The ground floor enclosed a cesspit; a garderobe emptied into the pit from a small first-floor chamber overhead. The second and third storeys still contain Tudor era modifications, as well as garderobes and arched windows. A fireplace on the third level retains its herringbone masonry and attractive lintel. Traces of the chimney also survive. A compact attic, which fills the uppermost storey, had a small square window.

Located on the south side of the keep and constructed over the ditch, the 14th-century middle gatehouse is now completely ruined. At first, the castle's main entrance would probably have been a simple archway like the one at Newcastle Bridgend, but, as defensive needs increased, so did the requirement for a more substantial gatehouse into the inner ward. The gate passage stretched only about 10 metres and was defended by a portcullis, a set of heavy wooden doors, and an arrowslit. A guardroom occupied the ground-level chamber, and access to the first floor was via a spiral staircase, fragments of which are visible.

Built by the de Turbervilles during the 14th century, the southern domestic range dominated the inner bailey. The now extensively ruined block of buildings once contained the great hall, a solar, and service buildings. Located in the centre of the ruins, the great hall occupied the first floor. It was reached through a vaulted passageway,

which can be identified by four large doorways, and climbing a massive spiral staircase. Another doorway also opened to a spiral staircase, which led to the basement and vaulted passageway of the structure originally planned as a chapel but never completed.

Extensively altered during the 16th century, the first-floor hall originally stood over a rib-vaulted undercroft. Three recessed windows offered views to the outside of the castle. A narrow, north-facing chamber held a fireplace and two other windows. Above the hall, private apartments contained a fine Tudor-era fireplace with herringbone masonry and two large windows. In addition to the dressed stone, several tombstones, undoubtedly taken from the adjoining church, adorned the walls. Along the outer wall, a round-fronted latrine tower projects southward into the ditch. It contained a vaulted cesspit in the basement, garderobes with small splayed windows on the three upper storeys, and a fireplace and an arrowslit on the top floor.

Just west of the hall, the service block contained the kitchen, pantry and buttery; fireplaces and ovens are still evident. A smaller building beyond the service block had additional fireplaces. The upper levels held living quarters, including the lord's solar. A brew-house stood between the kitchen and hall alongside the curtain wall; the square malting kiln retains its venting flues, the circular interior chamber, and a drain; remnants of a fireplace also survive.

The male line of the de Turbervilles died out with Richard de Turberville II in 1384, and Sir Lawrence Berkerolles acquired Coity Castle and associated estates by right of marriage to heiress Catherine de Turberville. Besides making repairs to the northern wall after Glyndwr's assault early in the 15th century, Sir Lawrence probably built the north-eastern gatehouse and began the chapel in the southern range mentioned above. He also converted several structures in the outer bailey and added the western gatehouse. Berkerolles intended his chapel for the first floor of an extension built onto the eastern side of the hall block. As indicated earlier, construction was never completed. Springers, a window with dressed Sutton stone, and what appears to be the altar mark the site.

The north-eastern gatehouse is one of the castle's finest features. Simple but useful, the rectangular structure still projects into the ditch. The two-storey gatehouse was defended by a single portcullis and fronted by a drawbridge. Spy holes (squints) were discreetly placed on the ground and first floor levels for defenders – and the Lords of Coity – to watch the action. A small room on the south-east side (possibly a guardroom?) was once accessed from the gate passage, but it has long since been blocked. The upper floors and the wall-walk were reached via a spiral staircase located at the opposite side of the passageway. A section of machicolated battlements survives. The upper levels were well equipped with garderobes; a fireplace heated the top chamber.

Sir Lawrence also converted the southern tower into a gatehouse, which probably contained a mill, and strengthened the western gatehouse. Inside the outer bailey, he erected a large, rectangular barn, which was accessed through a fine porch, the foundations of which line the wall adjacent to the southern gatehouse. An unusual set of eight arrowslits was embedded in the curtain wall at the rear of the barn, which must have been vulnerable to attack.

After Berkerolles' death in 1411, ownership of Coity Castle passed to the Gamage family, kinsmen of the de Turbervilles, who made the castle their primary residence in Glamorganshire. More than likely, Sir Thomas Gamage and his grandson, John, added the Tudor-era modifications to the castle to enhance the display of grace and comfort. In 1584, Barbara Gamage, heiress to the castle and to the Gamage fortune, married Sir Robert Sydney, Earl of Leicester, and the couple moved from Coity to Penshurst Place in Kent. The Sydneys neglected Coity Castle and it soon began to decay. Even though the castle remained the property of the Sydneys until the late 18th century, it was never restored. In 1811, it passed to the Earls of Dunraven, who turned the castle over to the State in 1929. For a time, the site may have been used as a farmyard and garden.

Cottrell

Some earthwork remains
Location: Contained within the golf course at Cottrell Park
near St. Nicholas, 6 miles east of Cowbridge along the A48
(ST 081 745)
Access: Only if you hit a wayward golf shot from near the 8th
tee! (N.B. the site can be seen from the way to St. Nicholas Gaer)

Cottrell is a flat-topped motte castle, the origins of which are unclear, as early medieval records do not specifically mention the site. However, historians believe it was located in the manor of Tre-hill as one of the three knights' fees of St. Nicholas. The other two fees, St. Nicholas and Coed-y-Cwm, were also based on timber castles; both are nearby.

The low-lying, circular mound sits on a glacial deposit, as was typical of Glamorgan's motte castles. Today, the motte rises only 1.7 metres high, but was probably taller when originally erected. Its diameter is approximately 20 metres. Though largely eroded, the encircling ditch is visible, except for a short stretch on the eastern side. Evidence for the existence of a bailey is scanty at best.

The association of the Cottrell name with the motte first dates conclusively to 1320, when Roger Cottrell owned the land. The castle itself was probably built by one of Roger's ancestors in the late 11th or early 12th century. A medieval manor house named Cottrell Court, also located in Tre-hill, may have replaced the motte when the owners needed a more substantial residence. It was in ruins by the 16th century. Cottrell Manor, a Tudor house, also stood on this estate, but it has long since been demolished.

Dinas Powys

Substantial stone remains, but very overgrown
Location: On the northern edge of Dinas Powys, itself between
Barry and Penarth (ST 153 717)
Access: A footpath provides access

Best approached from Lettons Way by the side of St. Peters Church on Mill Street in Dinas Powys, and then taking the path up the hillside on the right of the electricity sub-station. Even though the heavily ivy-clad ruins are difficult to full discern, the short trek is worth the time. New owners have plans to clear the site and make it easier for the public to access.

Probably replacing the earlier ringwork castle, the stone castle at Dinas Powys reflects the increased status of its builders, the de Somery (Sumeri) family. The new castle served as their caput until 1321, when the last male heir died. The simple design fits well on the steep-sided ridge-top. Running approximately north-west/south-east, the elongated castle featured an earthen embankment (a hornwork?) on the north-western edge of the ridge. The embankment extended around the western side of the site, but was truncated during the construction of the segmented curtain wall that enclosed the large rectangular ward. Interestingly, much of the north-western bank was destroyed by the on-site quarrying of Triassic limestone, which probably provided building material for the wall.

Archaeologists speculate that the north-western embankment may be evidence of the first castle at the site, and, therefore, date the structure to the early 12th century. The unusual structure was possibly erected to defend the square keep, which stood not too far to the south. Built at about the same time as the north-western embankment, the square Norman keep is extensively ruined. Evidently, much of the structural remains are buried beneath the earth and debris that have accumulated over the centuries.

Roger de Somery, a follower of Robert Fitzhamon, probably acquired the lordship of Dinas Powys soon after the Norman incursion into Glamorgan. Historical documents first mention the castle, 'Dinaspowis', in Ralph de Somery's will, which has been dated to 1203. After the death of William de Somery in 1222, the castle passed to Earl Gilbert de Clare. Apparently de Clare had intended to besiege the castle (some accounts say the siege had already begun).

Upon Richard de Clare's death in 1262, another Robert de Somery regained ownership of Dinas Powys Castle. The castle remained with the family until 1321, when John de Somery died.

The lordship was split between John's two sisters, Margaret Sutton and Joan de Botetourt, and the castle passed to the Suttons by right of marriage. In the 16th century, Sir Matthew Cradock acquired the stronghold, and it eventually passed to the Herbert Earls of Pembroke. Ultimately, Dinas Powys Castle fell into ruin.

In the 19th century, owner E.H. Lee carried out some restoration work, but it was not until 1979, when the local civic trust took a special interest in preserving the castle, that a deliberate effort was made to safeguard the site.

The walled bailey probably dates to the 13th century, and measures about 73 metres by 46 metres. Sections still rise to wall-walk level and stretch over two metres in width. Walls consist of rough stone and occasional tile and brick. Ashlar blocks were used at the corners and at some offsets along the length of walling. The north-eastern wall stands about six metres high and features a vaulted postern gate and numerous putlog holes. A large gap on the southern side probably pinpoints the location of the main gateway. Though little more than a ragged opening, it still has a drawbar hole. Besides enclosing the castle, the south-western segment of the western wall served as a revetment and bolstered the hillside to a depth of about four metres lower than the inner ward.

Dinas Powys ringwork

A series of overgrown banks and ditches
Location: Above a valley to the north-west of Dinas Powys
(ST 148 722)
Access: Can be reached by footpaths

Head along Mill Street and park in the small parking area on the
left just before crossing a small brook and opposite Millbrook
Road. Walk up the footpath signposted from this parking area,
which shadows a stream on the left, beyond which are the remains
of Dinas Powys Castle, and which then passes a number of large
greenhouses before emerging onto a track. Turn left on this track,
and then follow it round to the right as it heads up the next valley,
passing lines of beech trees on your right. At the end of these lines
of trees, and once the pathway has crossed a fence line, turn right
along the fence and follow a rougher path, which then turns left at
the crest of the ridge (which is also used by trail bikes) to reach the
series of banks and ditches that comprise the ringwork. The site is
heavily overgrown.

The tree-topped ringwork at Dinas Powys is, arguably, one of
Glamorgan's most enigmatic castles. More than likely the prede-

cessor to the stone castle of the same name which stands about ½ mile to the south-east, the earthwork castle was extensively excavated by the late Leslie Alcock in the 1950s. What makes the structure so unusual is the series of ramparts that line the site. Whereas most ringworks were defended by only one earthen bank and ditch, Dinas Powys features four parallel embankments. A fifth, probably unfinished, bank projects perpendicularly from the easternmost end of the outer rampart.

Beginning with the innermost earthwork, Alcock numbered the banks from 1 to 4. During excavations of bank number 2, he uncovered relics of early Christian masonry, including traces of two drystone walled houses, which associated this earliest portion of the site with the middle of the first millennium. More than likely, the inhabitants abandoned this early settlement in the 7th century. The few potsherds found in bank number 1 dated this structure to either the late 11th or early 12th century, when the de Somery (Sumeri) family owned the property.

The ringwork occupies the northern end of a promontory having steep drop-offs on all sides except the south, so it makes sense that the builders positioned the four embankments on that side to provide artificial strength. The innermost bank, number 1, featured a stone revetment; timber postholes uncovered during excavations along the cliff edge indicated the presence of what may have been an elevated fighting platform or possibly a timber tower. The outermost banks, numbers 3 and 4, were also fronted by deep ditches and stone revetments, and an unusual revetted causeway cut across bank 3 linked it to the inner embankments.

Two other embankments, labelled 'southern banks A and B', survive just south-west of the site. Archaeologists speculate that the southern bank, A, a straight embankment running north-east/south-west, may date to the Iron Age, whereas bank B, a V-shaped structure pointing towards the ringwork, may have been part of later siegeworks erected for an assault on the castle.

Dinas Powys ringwork probably served as the original caput for the de Somery family and may have been built by Roger de Somery in about 1100. Within a century, however, the de Somerys moved to the stronger stone castle nearby.

Ewenny Priory

Curtain walls, gatehouse and towers that guarded the priory
Location: 1 mile south of Bridgend (SS 913 778)
Access: Parts freely accessible, others incorporated
into a private house

To reach Ewenny Priory, take the A48 westerly from Cowbridge. Bear left on the B4524. Turn into a cluster of houses at the brown-and-white sign pointing to the 'historic 12th-century priory'. In less than a mile, you will reach the massive castellated walls of one of Wales' rare fortified monasteries.

Ewenny Priory rates more than a mention in this book on Glamorgan's castles because of its noteworthy fortified defences. In practice, it was a fairly minor Benedictine monastery begun in the early 12th century by William de Londres, who also founded nearby Ogmore Castle. Historical documents state that, between about 1115 and 1126, William de Londres established the original Norman church on the site, which apparently replaced an early church built by the Welsh. However, scholars still debate whether or not the present priory church was built by William, or by his son, Maurice, who is buried in the south transept. A decade after his father's death in 1131, Maurice de Londres affirmed the monks' ongoing use of the site by signing a 're-foundation charter'.

Today, Ewenny Priory is partly hidden behind dark medieval fortifications. Some portions survive intact, whereas others were incorporated into a later residence. The property is still occupied by the Picton Turbervill family, who maintain most of the site as a private home. One can gain a fine impression of the monastery's medieval grandeur by walking around the site and into the priory church, which is accessible throughout the year.

The western approach to Ewenny Priory is dominated by an imposing curtain wall, a massive gatehouse, and two strong towers which were constructed in the 13th and 14th centuries. These marked the precinct boundary. Impressive gatehouses became common features of such enclosing walls (see St. Davids Cathedral for example).

The northern and western sides of the site contain substantial remains of the battlemented precinct wall, which was added in the 13th century. The best preserved section of the perimeter wall measures about 69 metres in length and forms the western boundary. At one time, a ditch may have followed the wall, but it is no longer visible. Inside, a wall-walk runs along the upper level to the north-western tower. The massive round-fronted, partly battlemented tower controlled the northernmost end of the monastery; its arrows-lits (cross-oillets) are now blocked.

A well preserved length of 13th-century wall also runs between the north-western tower and the main gatehouse, a powerful-looking structure incorporating a portion of the earlier Norman gateway, one bay of which still faces into private property. Ironically, even though the battlemented gatehouse had what appeared to be twin octagonal towers with pyramidal angle spurs, the structures lacked arrowslits and consisted of little more than thick walls. Built of Carboniferous limestone, the northern gatehouse contains a variety of defensive features, including portcullis grooves and two square murder holes.

A spiral staircase hidden in the rectangular turret on the eastern wall of the gatehouse allowed medieval residents (defenders?) to reach the portcullis room located over the vaulted gate passage and also to access the wall-walk. Now, visitors can now only explore the ground floor. The room was fitted with a latrine chute that conveniently opened to the grounds outside the gatehouse, where water flowing through the ditch washed away the waste. During the 16th century, pigeonholes were added on the second storey to encourage breeding of the priory food supply; they are now only visible from outside the gatehouse.

Clearly smaller than its northern counterpart, the battlemented south gatehouse is viewable when standing at the inner end of the north gatehouse. Extensively remodelled shortly after 1300, it still contains both sections of the original Norman gateway and also retains a portcullis groove and murder holes. A two-storey tower added to the eastern side during the rebuilding phase features pyramidal angle spurs, trefoil and cinquefoil window heads, dressings of Sutton stone, a fireplace, and what seems to be a domed garderobe. A dungeon, reputedly hidden underneath the south gatehouse, still awaits excavation.

The southern section of curtain wall once linked the south gatehouse to the south-east tower (the 'columbarium'), but it was demolished during the 19th century to allow panoramic views of the countryside. A shorter eastern curtain wall, which also connected to the south-east tower, remains virtually intact. To see the tower, walk through the presbytery into the area just outside the church where the private family cemetery is located. Only a distant view of the tower is permitted, as the grounds are private and general access prohibited. Interestingly, the two-storey rectangular tower, which was built in the 1300s, was transformed into a large dovecote in the 16th century. Consequently, little of its medieval fabric survives. The priory brochure claims that the tower provided homes for over 1,000 birds and was 'perhaps the largest dovecote in Wales'.

At one time, another length of curtain walling completed the defensive circuit on the northern side. Now, only remnants remain of this wall, which joined the nave's western wall with the defences, lined the cemetery, and then ran to the powerful northern tower. Structurally similar to the main gatehouse, this battlemented tower still rises in part to first floor level. A south-facing doorway retains a drawbar hole and offers access to the barrel-vaulted basement level. Built in about 1300, the blocky tower had living quarters on its upper storey that could be accessed from the wall-walk. The first floor, not accessible to the public, contains remnants of a fireplace, a fine trefoil-headed window, and a latrine chute. Except for a very short length, the section of wall linking the north tower with the main gatehouse was demolished to make room for later structures, including the stone barn that now stands in its place.

Located amid the medieval walls, the Priory Church of St. Michael is actually quite large. From the exterior, a mammoth battlemented tower hints at its size, but the surrounding buildings encroach upon the cruciform church and create the impression that it is much smaller. Norman features can be identified both inside and out. The otherwise ruined north transept still displays a Norman (Romanesque) arch with skilfully-carved Norman zigzag designs; a carved head, perhaps a hound or a dragon, watches from above. Nearby, the simple doorway offers entry into the marvellous presbytery, the site of the high altar. Ribbed vaulting adorns the ceiling, and modern replicas of medieval tiles colour the floor.

The central tower and south transept dominate the church on the western side of the presbytery. Notable features include the tombs

of Maurice de Londres; his son, William; and great-granddaughter, Hawise de Londres. When Hawise died in 1274, the de Londres lineage died with her. Even though the vast estates passed to her son, Patrick de Chaworth, they soon went to the duchy of Lancaster, when Patrick's daughter, Maud, married the future King Henry IV. Effigies memorialise the Carne family and several grave slabs honour the de Turbervilles, whose descendants still own the estate. The south transept also contains some finely carved stones.

During restoration work completed in 2002, the decaying south transept was restored to its original Norman-era appearance. It acquired a new, watertight roof and a floor decorated with medieval tiles taken from the north transept. When conservators removed Victorian wall cement, they discovered an unusual band of bright purple paint, which may have formed part of a medieval mural painting. They also found several early Christian inscribed stones embedded in the walling, which have been placed on display alongside the medieval effigies.

Just after the dissolution of the monasteries in 1537, the Carnes leased Ewenny Priory and then purchased it outright eight years later. Sir Edward Carne promptly transformed the monastery into a grand residence, sometimes known as Mansion House, which incorporated several medieval structures, including the cloister and refectory. In 1741, the estate passed to Richard Turberville, son of the heiress to the Carne family fortune. In 1797, Richard Picton of Pembrokeshire, grandson and heir to Turberville's half-sister, acquired the property. He also adopted the surname 'Turbervill'. By then, the house had begun to decay, and it was up to Richard Picton Turbervill's descendants to restore it to a liveable condition. In 1949, the Picton Turbervills placed the monastic fortifications and the other medieval structures on the site into the guardianship of the State. The church remains in control of the parish and the rest of the estate is private.

Felin Isaf

Remains of motte and some ditching
Location: Just south of junction 34 on the M4 (ST 060 792)
Access: No public access

Sited on top a ridge of glacial drift, Felin Isaf motte was strate-gically placed at the edge of the natural scarp to watch over the activity on the River Ely, which flows nearby. Nothing about this castle has been found in historical documents. Some historians speculate that the castle may have been the caput of the Welsh lords of Meisgyn (Miskin) and held by them until 1247, when Richard de Clare defeated Hywel ap Maredudd and re-established a Norman power base at Llantrisant, a couple of miles to the north. Others believe the 3.4-metre high motte was a Norman-built stronghold.

Today, Felin Isaf is dwarfed by the modern Bosch factory built immediately to the north. Whereas the small but eroded motte has survived, the adjoining bailey has almost entirely disappeared. Portions of the original V-shaped ditch that defended the enclosure are clearly visible.

Fonmon Castle

A 13th-century castle much remodelled in the 1650s
and subsequently and still lived in
Location: 3 miles west of Barry (ST 047 681)
Access: Open for a fee between 1 April and 30 September on
Tuesday and Wednesday afternoons between 2pm and 5pm

The way to Fonmon Castle is signposted off the B4265 to the west of Fonmon village – you are asked not to approach the castle via Fonmon village as the roads are particularly narrow.

Fonmon Castle's austere, ivy-clad exterior belies the grandeur of its interiors where visitors may tour the hall, drawing room, library, and kitchen during summer months. Now well disguised behind exquisite plasterwork and post-medieval panelling, the medieval castle survives in part inside the modern structure but is virtually impossible to detect. The site is particularly noteworthy for having been constantly occupied, albeit extended and remodelled, since its inception, which probably occurred in the late 12th century. The present owner, Sir Brook Boothby, is a direct descendant of Colonel Philip Jones, who purchased the castle from its original owners, the St. John family, in 1656. Sir Brook maintains the property and surrounding landscape in tiptop condition, and the castle looks essentially as it did in the 1760s, when it underwent a final refurbishment programme.

Historians once claimed that the first owner of Fonmon manor was Oliver St. John, a comrade of Robert Fitzhamon, who acquired the estate in 1091. They now believe this story to be myth, and set a later date of 1200 for the arrival of the first St. Johns. In the late 13th century, Sir William II was the first St. John recorded as Lord of Fonmon; however, it is likely that the actual builder of the castle was Sir William I, who was active in Glamorgan from the late 12th to mid-13th century. More than likely, the elder William built a rectangular stone keep, which became the medieval core of the castle. Speculation exists that the keep fronted an even earlier earthwork castle, but nothing survives to support this notion.

Originally, the keep had 5-metre thick walls and featured a basement and two upper storeys. It may have been flanked on its southern side by a ditch, but that has long since been built over. A splendid rococo library/drawing room now occupies the first floor. Notable features in this room, added by Robert Jones III during the last building phase in the 1760s, include an elaborate plasterwork ceiling, broad, floral designs, hunting themes, and other ornamentation. The room above the library now serves as a bedroom and has panelling added by Col. Philip Jones in the 1660s.

Immediately to the east of the keep stands the north-east tower, which has a rounded corner on the south-east and a squared extension to the north. Probably added by Sir William St. John II or Alexander St. John during the third building phase, the tower not only offered access between the levels of the keep but also held latrines. Projecting southward, a length of curtain wall, which probably just predates the tower, formed the eastern side of a courtyard. The inner ward was further enclosed by the keep, a battlemented eastern range of buildings (dating to the 17th century), the south range, and the south-east tower. A western wall once completed the courtyard circuit, but it no longer survives.

The three-storey south-east tower probably provided additional living quarters as well as enhanced defensive strength. A southern extension offered added protection for the new south range, which had latrines, several small rooms (still in fine repair), and a small fireplace on its two levels. Stairs led to the rooftop, which was embellished with sham battlements in the 19th century. The south range now contains a large drawing room, original 19th-century plasterwork, and sham battlements.

From the early 15th century until the castle's sale to Col. Jones, the St. Johns leased the property to several people, including members of the Basset family – who owned Old Beaupre Castle among other sites – and minor members of the St. John family. In the mid-17th century, Sir Oliver St. John (5th Baron St. John of Bletsoe and 2nd Earl of Bolingbroke) found himself in such dire financial straits that he was forced to sell the castle and his other Glamorganshire properties. Since then, the castle has remained with the Joneses and their descendants.

Col. Jones was a staunch Parliamentarian who played a key role in Cromwell's Protectorate. Besides being governor of Cardiff Castle, and the high sheriff of Glamorgan, Jones served as Comptroller for Cromwell's household and organised the Lord Protector's funeral in 1658. Even though Col. Jones instigated a major rebuilding programme at Fonmon Castle, he spent most of his time away on other business and leased out the castle. In 1662, after the lease ran out, he built a substantial, three-storey block of buildings, which completely engulfed the medieval stronghold and the north annexe erected in the late 16th century. Besides living quarters, the north block contained a dairy, laundry, scullery, and an enormous kitchen, said to be the largest of its kind in Britain.

During the 1760s, Robert Jones III added the final touches to Fonmon Castle. Much of the modern interiors, including the lavish library/drawing room and the castellation of the exterior of the castle, was his handiwork. He also revamped the grounds, built the folly watchtower, added new sash windows, transformed the medieval barn into a stable block, and remodelled the eastern range into an impressive staircase hall. Since then, only minor changes and repairs have been made to the castle.

In 1917, the male line of the Jones family died out, and the castle passed by right of marriage first to Robert Valpy and then to Clara Valpy, whose husband was Sir Seymour Boothby, ancestor of the current owner, Sir Brook Boothby.

Gelligaer
(Twyn Castell)

> A motte
> Location: About 100 metres east of the parish church
> in Gelligaer, itself south-west of Bargoed (ST 137 969)
> Access: Although on private ground, it can be seen
> from several points on the surrounding roads

Gelligaer is located on the B4254, which can be accessed via the A469 south-west of Bargoed. Look for the parish church, parts of which date to the 13th and 16th centuries. Park nearby. The motte, which is now part of several private gardens, is about 100 metres east of the church but can be seen from the surrounding roads.

This is one of the few motte castles in Glamorganshire likely to have been erected by the Welsh. The tree-covered motte may have been the so-called *Castrum Cadwallon* (or 'Cadwallon's Castle'), which served as caput of the Welsh Lords of Senghennydd in the 12th and 13th centuries. The roughly circular motte has steep sides that originally rose at least seven to ten metres high. Its basal diameter is about 32 metres across. The summit stretches 18 metres and supports a few trees.

Only 150 metres to the north-west, the ruins of the Roman fort of the same name can also be explored.

Gelli Garn
(St. Mary Hill)

> Scant earthwork remains
> Location: On the north of St. Mary Hill,
> 3 miles east of Bridgend (SS 960 787)
> Access: Can be seen from adjacent public footpath

Turn north off the A48 in Pentre Meyrick and keep ahead on the minor road which, after about a mile and a half will lead you into a 40mph limit. Just before the end of this limit, turn left to St. Mary Hill. Keep right at the Y-shaped split in the road, and immediately after another road off to the left, park at the start of the farm track on the right. You'll see a footpath sign pointing up this track, which you walk up towards the farm. The remains, such as they are, are in the field on the left below the farmhouse.

Although the OS map labels the site as a 'motte & bailey', the castle at Gelli Garn is actually a modest ringwork and bailey which has been greatly eroded by ploughing. Consequently, it is a bit difficult to identify. The circular ringwork stood only 1.5 metres high; its summit stretched abut 25 metres. Until recently, the entire perimeter was encircled by a ditch, which now survives only on the eastern side. Immediately east of the ringwork, vestiges of the original rectangular bailey are still visible, although they too have been damaged by ploughing.

While nothing is known of the original occupants of the castle, the site probably served as the caput for the sub-fee of Gelli Garn. In the late 12th century, Samson de Hawey granted the ringwork to Neath Abbey in exchange for use of the abbey's vill at Littleham, near Bideford in Devon. Apparently, de Hawey's finances were in such disarray that he was forced to make the exchange and move away.

Granville's Castle

Historical documents from 1129 indicate that a motte castle existed on the western bank of the River Neath (Nedd) prior to the construction of the stone castle on the opposite bank. Erected by Richard de Granville, reputed to have been Robert Fitzhamon's brother, the now-vanished castle sat fairly close to Granville's greater achievement, Neath Abbey. Whereas the abbey survives in ruin, nothing remains of the castle except the site, which is located in the midst of a housing estate and school fields. Here, in about 75 AD, the Romans built *Nidum*, an auxiliary fort which controlled traffic along the river. It was abandoned during the 2nd century.

Richard de Granville's castle served as the caput of his minor lordship, which covered the westernmost fringes of Glamorganshire during the early 12th century. Granville granted his castle and estates to the Cistercian monks at Neath Abbey upon his retirement in 1130, at which time he moved to Devon. By 1207, the castle had already disappeared from historical records, having probably been demolished by the monks.

Gwern-y-Domen

Ringwork remains
Location: Half a mile east of Caerphilly (ST 175 878)
Access: Well trodden disued railway line leads to the site

From the roundabout on the A468 on the north-western edge of Caerphilly, take the minor road that is signposted to Rudry, soon turning left again following the signs to Rudry. Follow this road for about half a mile, parking where a metalled track leads off to the right and across a bridge over the disused railway line. Walk up this track to the bridge, then drop down onto the old railway line and walk back along it towards Caerphilly. The track passes right by the castle remains in a few hundred yards.

Labelled as a 'mound' on the OS map, Gwern-y-Domen ('the marsh of the mound') overlooks the River Rhymni from atop a glacial hillock, like most of Glamorgan's motte castles. Also like so many of Glamorgan's motte castles, nothing is known of the site's history. From a distance, the structure looks like a truncated motte, but closer examination reveals that a fairly substantial embankment rims the oval mound. The site is actually a ringwork, and probably dates to the early 12th century. The southern side was extensively damaged when a railway was constructed alongside the castle.

The ringwork features a dished out centre, which stretches approximately 25 metres across. The embankments rise about five metres high and are tallest on the southern and eastern sides. To the west, the original entry onto the summit is still identifiable. A series of what appear to be water-filled ditches and counterscarps are also visible on the eastern side of the ringwork. A few trees stand in what may have been the bailey on the western side of the castle.

Howe Mill Enclosure

No obviously visible remains
Location: 2 miles south-east of Cowbridge (ST 005 721)
Access: The public footpath that leads to Beaupre Castle
(see above) passes on the other side of the stream from the site

Follow the instruction as for reaching Beaupre Castle. As you walk along the footpath towards Beaupre Castle, look to the right, tracing the river for any evidence of the earthen embankment. The author was unable to detect any remains.

Originally the crescent-shaped earthen embankment faced a natural escarpment which fell to the River Thaw. Whereas the river still flows through the area, virtually nothing survives of the partial ringwork due to rigorous ploughing. During the 12th century, the partial ringwork may have served as the caput for the knight's fee of Llandough. It was probably replaced by the larger tower house in Llandough.

Kenfig

Some fairly overgrown masonry remains
Location: In the sand dunes about halfway between Port Talbot
and Bridgend (SS 801 826)
Access: Can be reached on foot through the dunes

Park near Mawdlam Church. Head towards the fence at the foot of the M4 embankment and follow this to gate in a fenceline. Once through this, if you turn half-left you should be able to see the scant stone remains of Kenfig Castle above some scrub about ¼ mile away, with a small field as a backdrop. Take any of the various paths through the dunes to reach the castle.

Earl Robert FitzRoy probably selected this spot to build a castle for two reasons. First was its proximity to the River Cynffig, which has long since receded from the site as the dunes have evolved over time. The river once served as the castle's moat and flowed around its northern and western sides. The site was also located near the *Via Julia Maritima* (the Port Way), which the Romans built as a major communications route between their forts at Cardiff and Neath. FitzRoy probably used the same road for ease of movement through the area. During the 1140s, Kenfig became the administrative centre, or caput, for the minor lordship of Margam and continued to play a key role in regional politics until the 15th century, when the sands encroached upon the site.

Positioned as the westernmost outpost of the Glamorgan lordship and adjacent to the lordship of Afan, Kenfig Castle and its associated borough experienced several assaults by the Welsh. They occurred in 1167; 1183-84 (led by Morgan ap Caradog); 1228 (led by Hywel ap Maredudd); 1232 (led by Morgan Gam); 1243 (led by Hywel ap Maredudd); 1295 (led by Morgan ap Maredudd); and 1316 (possibly led by Llywelyn Bren). On each occasion, the town was burned or destroyed; but, only in 1232 and 1295 did the Welsh inflict enough serious damage to the castle to require significant repairs.

Speculation still exists over the exact nature of FitzRoy's castle. More than likely, the Norman castle was a ringwork; however, no physical evidence survives to support this notion. Shortly after completing the putative ringwork, builders very definitely added a stone keep measuring about 14 metres square and with walls about 3.7 metres thick. Access was through a gateway on the southwestern side of the site.

In the late 13th century, Gilbert de Clare extensively altered Kenfig Castle, probably in response to the devastation caused by the Welsh. He raised the height of the inner bailey almost to the keep's first-floor level and erected a polygonal stone curtain wall to replace the timber ramparts. The new wall was primarily used to revet the raised level of the interior. De Clare also completely reconstructed the southern wall of the keep and added vaulting to the basement ceiling, which partially blocked one of the arrowslits. A fairly plain rectangular gatehouse was added on the southwestern side immediately opposite the keep.

In 1321, Marcher barons revolted against Hugh le Despenser, Lord of Glamorgan. Joining forces with the Welsh, they attacked Kenfig for an eighth time. Borough and castle were completely destroyed, as were many of Despenser's other castles in Glamorganshire, but both borough and castle at Kenfig were rebuilt by the end of the century. Besides expanding the gatehouse, the

Despensers constructed a rectangular building on the southern wall adjacent to the main gate; its function is unclear. Excavations have revealed that another rectangular structure may also have stood on the northern side of the inner ward. The Despensers also replaced the basement doorway in the keep with a lavish version faced with Sutton stone.

Kenfig was notable not just for its castle but also for the associated medieval town, mentioned above, which the dunes now obscure close to the south-western side of the castle. Historical records indicate that Kenfig was incorporated in 1147 and that St. James Church was founded by 1151. The earliest surviving borough charter dates to 1397. The borough was managed by the castle's constable and a portreeve. By 1307, 700 to 800 people lived in the borough, which operated water and windmills and maintained a leper hospital and guildhall. Portions of the enclosing earthen ramparts reputedly still trace the town's boundary. During the 15th century, the shifting dunes almost entirely overwhelmed the original church. Consequently, worshippers moved the stones to a new site at nearby Pyle, where they re-erected the building. The castle was abandoned soon afterwards.

In 1989, the Kenfig Society was formed to study and document the remains of the medieval borough. Since 1993, members have undertaken annual excavations of sections of the town site. Their considerable finds include medieval coins, pottery, bone, shells, iron slag, and a medieval rubbish dump. Prehistoric and Roman-era finds, including tiles and coins, have also been unearthed. Substantial ruins of a building of uncertain use together with medieval agricultural furrows have been excavated.

Llanblethian
(St. Quintin's, St. Quentin's)

Some stonework remains
Location: South of the A48 in Cowbridge (ST 989 742)
Access: In the care of Cadw, open most days from
11am to dusk, no charge

From Cowbridge town centre, take Church Street southward to Town Mill Road, which becomes Constitution Hill and curves to the right onto Castle Hill. Alternatively, take Broadway west to Castle Hill and drive briefly north to the castle.

Dominating the western end of a ridge overlooking the River Thaw, Llanblethian Castle was ideally situated to watch over the region. The naturally sloping hill gave the inhabitants added protection on three fronts, and two large corner towers and the substantial gatehouse fortified the most vulnerable eastern side. Today, the towers barely rise above ground level. The northernmost tower is still attached to the gatehouse by a section of curtain wall; shrubbery obscures the other tower. The low-lying walls of the quadrangular castle project outward from the corner towers and the western side connects to another wall. A gap in the northern wall may be all that remains of a postern gate. The irregularities in the grassy hillside area just outside the northern curtain wall (adjacent to the small car park) indicate that additional buildings once stood at the site.

More than likely, Herbert de St. Quintin built the first castle at Llanblethian at the start of the 12th century. Probably a ringwork, like so many others in this region, the earth-and-timber fortification would have been replaced by the stone keep, which now lies in ruin

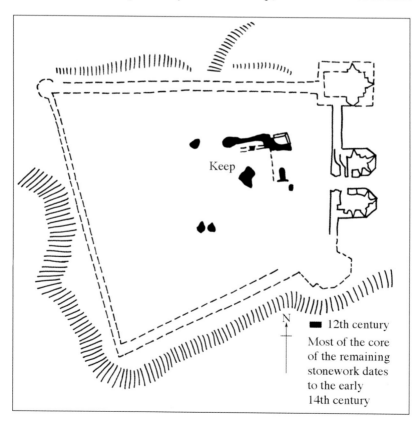

Keep

N

■ 12th century

Most of the core
of the remaining
stonework dates
to the early
14th century

inside the inner bailey about 5 metres beyond the massive gatehouse. Reputedly once one of Glamorgan's largest, the keep is now essentially a pile of rubble and stone; pieces of a straight staircase can be identified amongst the remains.

The St. Quintin family controlled much of this part of the Vale of Glamorgan during the 12th and 13th centuries. Their main rivals were the Siwards, with whom they intermarried and then shared property. Besides Llanblethian Castle, the St. Quintins and Siwards owned castles in Glamorganshire at Talyfan, Ystradowen and Llanilid, and also in England. In 1233, Richard Siward forced John de St. Quintin to give up his Welsh properties, and the St. Quintins promptly abandoned the castle at Llanblethian. Siward continued to control his Glamorgan estates until 1245, but he used Talyfan rather than Llanblethian as his base. After unwisely choosing to side with the Welsh against Richard de Clare, Siward was declared an outlaw and had his properties seized by the Lord of Glamorgan. Richard Siward died in 1248, and Llanblethian Castle remained with the de Clares.

From 1307 to 1314, Gilbert de Clare III revamped Llanblethian Castle, refurbishing the keep, extending the castle's defences and constructing a new gatehouse. Even though the gatehouse is a ruin, its size and carefully dressed stonework still impress; its two polygonal towers dominate each side of the gate passage. Inside, remnants of original ribbed archways, murder holes, cross-oillets (modified arrowslits), and two portcullises are still visible. Guardrooms filled the ground floors of both towers. First floor chambers above the guardrooms held accommodation and a large central chamber also dominated the level. Surviving features include the remains of a fireplace, a latrine lit by another cross-oillet, and portions of the wall-walk.

By the time of Gilbert III's death at the Battle of Bannockburn, only a portion of the gatehouse had been completed. Subsequently, the curtain walls were never raised to a defensible height and the ditch was only partially excavated. In 1321, Llanblethian and several other castles in Glamorganshire were burned during the barons' rebellion against Hugh le Despenser, Lord of Glamorgan. Afterwards, Despenser repaired Llanblethian Castle. During the

15th century, it became a significant administrative centre for the neighbouring borough of Cowbridge, and, for some time, the castle was actually known as Cowbridge Castle.

By the 1470s, Llanblethian Castle was in use as a prison. Then, during the 16th century, ownership passed to the Crown, and the castle was then granted to William Herbert, later the Earl of Pembroke. In the 1680s, the castle's constable also served as the mayor of the borough of Cowbridge. By the mid-1700s, however, the structure was documented as a ruin. During the 19th century, it housed livestock. Fortunately, Cadw finally took over care of the site and began consolidating the ruins and restoring the gatehouse. The castle was opened to the public in 2001.

Llandaff

Now largely a walled garden,
an impressive gatehouse still survives
Location: Adjacent to Llandaff Cathedral (ST 156 780)
Access: Freely accessible at any reasonable time

To reach Llandaff Castle, take the lane off the A4119 that heads towards Llandaff Cathedral. Parking for the bishops' castle can be found in front of the ruined medieval bell tower, which dates to the 13th century but now forms part of the Llandaff war memorial. Both sites are freely accessible at any reasonable time.

While not specifically built to guard the river crossing, Llandaff Castle was situated to overlook the River Taff. The castle actually provided defensive strength for the bishops who served at Llandaff Cathedral, just a few hundred metres to the north. From the castle, they could watch over activity in the cathedral precinct and rush there (or prepare to defend themselves) if necessary.

Compared to many castles, Llandaff Bishops' Castle is very simplistic in plan. However, although some historians label the site as a 'palace', its thick walls, twin-towered gatehouse, harsh façade, and strong overall plan qualify it as a true castle. Probably built in the 1270s by Bishop William de Braose, whose relatives were Lords of Gower, Llandaff Castle has affinities with the larger Edwardian castles being constructed at about the same time. Quite possibly, nearby Caerphilly Castle inspired de Braose to build a similar gatehouse at Llandaff, albeit on a much smaller scale.

The main gatehouse is Llandaff Castle's most impressive feature. Short pyramidal spurs support the bases of two squat gate towers, which held a prison in the eastern tower and guardrooms and living chambers in the west. At one time, the uppermost levels of the towers connected midway over the gate passage. Defensive features inside the gate passage included an arrowslit, a portcullis and heavy timber doors. The tall rectangular turret projecting southward from the western gate tower held the spiral stair that gave access to upper levels. Today, visitors may peer inside the western tower through the arrowslit located in the vaulted passage.

Unlike the western side of the gate passage, which opened into a guardroom and was heated by a fireplace, the eastern side was starkly furnished. Entry into the east tower could be achieved only from inside the courtyard, the doorway from which is now barred. The tower also lacked arrowslits.

From the interior, the castle's garden setting masks its medieval might. The thick battlemented curtain wall stood at least 5 metres high, supported a wall-walk, and connected the towers and hall block. Today, the best preserved section of wall survives on the south-east. A large square tower on the south side of the inner courtyard projected outward from the wall and a smaller round eastern tower also defended the site. Presently barred, both towers contained at least one fireplace, garderobes and windows. An arched doorway partly protruding from ground level of the eastern tower once offered access to a basement. Now only represented by a large gap in the curtain wall and a tall window, the completely ruined hall block would have been an impressive sight in its heyday. The great hall and solar occupied the upper floor, where a small chapel annexe projected outward from the solar.

Llandaff Castle had a relatively peaceful history. While some historical documents indicate that Owain Glyndwr devastated the castle in about 1404, no firm evidence supports this notion. In fact, the Bishops of Llandaff continued to reside inside the formidable structure until the middle of the 15th century, when they moved to Mathern Palace in Monmouthshire. Control of the castle then passed to the Mathew family, who held the site until 1818, when Sir Samuel Romilly purchased the manor and castle of Llandaff.

By the 1770s, Llandaff Castle had fallen into ruin. The Bush Inn ale house had been erected against the eastern gate tower, and a similar structure stood to the west of the castle. By the mid-19th century, the inn was gone and the castle courtyard had been transformed into a walled garden for the bishop's enjoyment. In the 1970s, the Church acquired the property, consolidated the ruins, and opened the site to the public as a walled garden.

Despite extensive restoration after Second World War bombing destroyed much of the site, neighbouring Llandaff Cathedral retains some of its medieval craftsmanship, including the tombs of several members of the Mathew family and Bishop William de Braose, the gilded shrine of St. Teilo, and the lovely Lady Chapel, also the work of William de Braose. On the outside, fine medieval carvings adorn the spires.

Llandough

The remains are being restored as a major mansion
Location: In the centre of the settlement of Llandough,
1 mile south of Cowbridge (SS 995 730)
Access: The mansion can be glimpsed from parts of the
lanes in the vicinity

Park near the 12th- to 13th-century parish church which stands above an array of white-painted modern houses, walk back to the letter box and turn right up the lane to reach the castle. Visitors can stroll around part of the perimeter, where the revamped gatehouse is the highlight of the walk.

Fairly well hidden behind a high stone wall, Llandough Castle is a private residence, its earliest structural remains embedded within later modifications. Yet, enough survives within view to hint at the grandeur that once made this one of Glamorgan's finest tower houses.

The knight's fee of Llandough appears in historical records as early as the 12th century, but it was not until the 15th century that a tower house was built here. An earthwork castle, perhaps a ringwork or a simple stone castle, may have originally graced the spot where the castle presently stands; alternatively, it may have stood even closer to the church. Whichever place the earliest castle once occupied, sadly, nothing has survived. That castle would have served as the fee's caput, or administrative centre. The lords of Llandough, members of the prolific Walsh family (variant spellings: Walsche, Walshe, Walensis, Wallensis, Wales, Waleys, Waleis), occupied the fine fortified residence until the 1440s. They probably built the original tower house.

In 1444, Payn de Van sold Llandough Castle to Sir William ap Thomas (Herbert), Earl of Pembroke and owner of Raglan Castle in Monmouthshire. The Herberts eventually passed the property to their successors, the Somersets, Earls of Worcester, when Elizabeth, the Herbert heiress, married Sir Charles Somerset. Both families had interests elsewhere and appointed a bailiff to manage their estates in Glamorganshire. Consequently, they neglected Llandough Castle, and by the 1530s, when John Leland visited the site, it lay in ruins.

In 1536, Henry Somerset, 2nd Earl of Worcester, sold Llandough Castle to Sir Edward Carne, whose brother, William, served as the castle's bailiff. For a time, Sir Edward lived at the castle, having restored it. However, he also occupied Ewenny Priory, and his participation in the dissolution of the monasteries took him away from home. In 1685, the castle passed to Martha Carne and her husband, Sir Edward Mansel, who owned the grand estates at Penrice, Oxwich, and Margam, where he preferred to live. By the turn of the century, the tower house had been leased to a series of farming tenants, who continued to allow the site to decay.

In 1750, when the last male heir to the Mansel line died childless, the estate at Llandough passed to an heiress, Mary, and her husband, John Ivory Talbot of Lacock Abbey, Wiltshire. Their son, Thomas, renamed himself Mansel Talbot and continued to lease Llandough Castle to various tenants. Tenant Edward Mathew of Aberamman greatly improved the quality of life at Llandough: by 1757, the residence offered fine accommodation serviced by a brewery, pigeon house, dairy and kitchen, a barn, stables, coach house, wagon house, a kiln, pleasure gardens – and a bowling green. Within 50 years, however, Llandough Castle had become extensively ruined.

The late medieval structure at Llandough actually consisted of a rectangular tower house, a gatehouse, and ancillary buildings (the hall block), which faced into the huge square courtyard. Thirteen-metre tall crenellated walls enclosed the courtyard. At one time, the exterior of the site was also surrounded by a ditch, long since in-filled, into which latrine chutes dumped. Most of the structure was probably built by Robert Walsh, the last male of his lineage, or by Elizabeth, his widow, and her second husband, John Van, Lord of Marcross, during the 15th century.

Today, only portions of the tower house, a length of walling on the north-east side of the enclosure, and the gatehouse survive to any degree. Probably a typical example of its kind, the tower house once stood on the north-western side of the site. Even though the later mansion incorporated most of it, the garderobe turret is still identifiable at the southern end of the house.

Constructed in the 16th century, the gatehouse was actually a rebuilding of a medieval angle tower that stood at the southern corner of the courtyard. In many ways, the gatehouse itself resembles a tower house. Now a residence, the structure features a tall gabled roof line, a narrow turret projecting eastward in line with the curtain wall, windows on all three levels, putlog holes, and arrows-lits, all of which existed on the medieval gateway, the exact location of which remains uncertain. Even though most of the interior was rather plain, its walls were faced with dressed stone, the windows had mouldings and mullions, and fireplaces would have allowed for heat to the upper storeys. An Elizabethan archway still frames the main entrance.

The hall range, which once stood along the north-eastern wall, still features several recesses. Three fireplaces, doors, and passages suggest the presence of the kitchen and service range. The hall itself was probably located on the level above, where remnants of a fireplace also survive. Sometime later, pigeonholes were introduced into the recesses, which may have initially held large windows but are now blocked.

Across the lane on the southern side of Llandough Castle, several revamped homes once served the lords inside the curtain wall. Their names – the Stables, the Mews – suggest their original relationships with the tower house and give insight into the overall layout of the estate.

Most of the present site dates to a major rebuilding programme initiated by John Price in the early 19th century, which transformed the decaying 'castle' into a grand residence. Although Price did not actually own Llandough Castle, he made extensive improvements to the ageing structure, adding parlours on the ground floor, a first-floor drawing room, and a wing on the eastern side for the servants' quarters.

After Price's death in 1818, other tenants leased Llandough Castle. In 1890, Sir Sidney Hutchinson Byass bought the site, but upon his death in 1929, the estate fell into disarray. The servants' quarters were demolished and outbuildings were left to decay until 1970, when the house was purchased by the Andersons, who have since renovated the site and made it liveable.

Inside the nearby church, the medieval relics and graves of personalities associated with the castle, such as Gwenllian Walsh (d.1427) and Joan Carne (d.1628), are viewable.

Llandow

Only barest traces of castle site
Location: Just south of the church in Llandow, itself 3 miles
south-west of Cowbridge (SS 942 732)
Access: Site lies alongside a public footpath

Llandow is best accessed by taking the B4270 north from Llantwit Major, turning left about 2 miles onto a minor lane to Llandow. Park near Holy Trinity Church and walk south on the public footpath immediately across from the church, after only a short distance crossing a stone stile to then shadow the fence on your left. At this point the castle site, such as it is, will be on your right.

According to the historical record, Llandow was a knight's fee held by the Winton family for the service of a single knight. Once located in the open field behind the houses opposite the churchyard, the site is now virtually non-existent, thanks to extensive ploughing and the encroachment of more recent housing and road construction. A barn, tall grass, and rusting farm equipment litter the site.

Potsherds discovered here reliably date the castle to the 12th century, and fragments of a 13th-century wall indicate the site was probably occupied for at least a century. Remnants of an associated medieval settlement, including earthworks for several crofts, a mill pond, and a house site, also survive.

You can also visit the attractive church, which contains a Norman nave and chancel and other features dating from the 13th through to the 15th centuries.

Llangynwyd

Some stone fragments and earthworks remain
Location: 1 mile south of Maesteg (SS 652 887)
Access: Well hidden in woodland and undergrowth
on private land

The castle at Llangynwyd lies to the west of the village, near a junction of streams. Whilst not far from a minor road, it is impossible to see any remains from the thoroughfare. Permission must be sought from the property owner to reach the site.

At one time, Llangynwyd must have been an impressive sight. Today, it is debris-covered and so well disguised under trees that it is essentially inaccessible to the public. The only excavations at the site were conducted in 1906. Surface indications reveal the presence of several masonry structures, including what may have been one of Gilbert de Clare II's finest gatehouses. The remains are on private property west of the village, but are accessible. Fragments from the castle are embedded in the porch of the parish Church of St. Cenydd, which stands in the centre of Llangynwyd village and dates at least to the 13th century.

Situated on the top of a promontory at the northern edge of Forestry Commission land, the castle site consists of two distinct areas: a broad bailey at the north-west and a D-shaped inner ward enclosed by earthen embankments, where the main castle stood, possibly on the site of the original ringwork erected in the 12th century. Speculation exists that the stone castle may have been built by the Welsh, but, more than likely, Robert FitzRoy, Earl of Gloucester and Lord of Glamorgan, seized the stronghold. Sometimes known as Castell Coch, the castle served as the caput of Tir yr Iarll (Earl's Land), an upland area between the rivers Garw and Afan.

In 1257, Llywelyn ap Gruffydd stormed and burned Llangynwyd Castle and killed most of the garrison. Even though Richard de Clare continued to maintain a constable at Llangynwyd, he apparently made no effort to repair the site. During 1262, Humphrey de Bohun managed the lordship of Glamorgan for the underage heir, Gilbert de Clare II. He attempted to restrengthen the castle and possibly erected the curtain wall on the banks of the ringwork. As an adult, Gilbert undertook a major rebuilding programme and transformed Llangynwyd into a fairly formidable fortress. It was assaulted by the Welsh in the late 13th or early 14th century and abandoned shortly thereafter.

A deep ditch and bank still surround the inner ward on all but the north-eastern side, where a steep natural slope offered ample protection from an attack. On the western side, a crescent-shaped embankment defended the main entrance. Beyond, remnants of the twin-towered gatehouse survive, albeit disguised by years of weathering, neglect and overgrowth. The interior of the castle is difficult to interpret, since the site has yet to be cleared or consolidated. To the north, vestiges of a round tower are barely visible. Along the eastern wall, remnants of what may have been a large great hall and its service block can be distinguished. Another long building of uncertain purpose may have also stood on the opposite side of the inner bailey.

During the later 13th century, the fine gatehouse undoubtedly dominated the site; however, the stronghold at Llangynwyd was no match for Welsh rebels led by Morgan ap Maredudd, who burned the castle in 1294. Control of Tir Iarll moved to Kenfig Castle, and Llangynwyd Castle was abandoned and forgotten until 1906. In excavations undertaken that year, Frederick Evans documented much about the defensive capabilities of the gatehouse, which included arrowslits, portcullises, and double doors, whilst guardrooms flanked the gate passage.

Llanilid

Substantial remains of a ring-motte or raised ringwork
Location: 4 miles east of Bridgend (SS 977 813)
Access: Freely accessible by public footpath

Take the M4 to exit 35, and head north on the A473 towards Pencoed. Turn right at the roundabout on the road to Felindre and Llanilid. After about a mile turn left onto a lane signposted to Llanilid. This soon narrows and you follow it to a three-way split where the left hand branch heads to a farm. You want to park here and then walk through the gate on the right just before the split where a finger post points to the church. A track leads to the church and the prominent castle mound now clad in trees.

Llanilid is a fine example of what has been variously labelled a 'ring-motte', a 'raised ringwork', and, simply enough, a 'ring-work', for this fascinating site features characteristics of both types of earth and timber castle. However, it most strongly resembles a motte with a bank ringing the summit, and, therefore, is best identified as a ring-motte.

The tree-covered undulating mound sits atop a glacial hillock alongside Llanilid's Church of St. Ilid and St. Curig. Across the lane to the parish church, a slender stream trickles through the trees and may once have served as the castle's water supply. Accessible on foot for almost its entire perimeter, the elongated mound is surrounded on all but its eastern side by a ditch, which is partly water-filled. On the south side, which points towards the church, a cleft in the mound probably marks the site of the original entrance onto the ringwork.

Only when on top can one comprehend why this tall, circular mound should be characterised as a ring-motte rather than either a motte or a ringwork. What makes Llanilid unusual is the height of the earthwork ring that rims the top of the mound. While standing inside the castle on its summit, which stretches about 30m in diameter, one has the sensation of being in a shallow crater, for the ringed embankment rises another one to two metres above the inner level of the mound. On the exterior, the steeply sloping sides seem to plunge perilously to ground level and emphasise how useful these embanked castles were for watching for approaching attackers and welcome visitors, and also for impeding an onslaught. The embankment would have supported timber palisades.

During the 12th century, Llanilid was part of the caput of Rhuthin. Located between the lordships of Coity and Talyfan, Rhuthin was the third of the lordships established when Earl Robert of Gloucester severed Morgannwg into the Welshry (Blaenau Morgannwg) in the uplands and the Englishry (Bro Morgannwg) in the more fertile coastal areas. The lordship of Rhuthin covered the parishes of Llanharan, Llanilid and St. Mary Hill. The three lordships were held by Norman lords 'with royal liberty', able to rule with almost regal power.

Llanilid was held by the Welsh until about 1130, when they turned the property over to Neath Abbey. The St. Quintins, who owned nearby Castell Talyfan, promptly gained control of the parish and surrounding lands and turned over the management of their holdings to the Siward family. The Siwards, who had married St. Quintin heiresses and became prosperous by right of marriage, probably built Llanilid Castle shortly thereafter. They continued to control the site until 1245, when Richard de Clare seized their properties after they had sided with the Welsh.

From then onward, Llanilid Castle remained the possession of the lords of Glamorgan. More than likely, the Siwards retreated to the moated site at **Gadlys** (SS 979 812), which exists some 200 metres south-south-east of the ringwork. This poorly preserved moated site may have served as the caput of the sub-lordship of Rhuthin (in the hands of the St. Quintins). From there, the Siwards would have continued their role as stewards to the Lord of Glamorgan. Only scant remains survive of the moated site, including heavily eroded embankments on all but the northern side of the rectangular site and, possibly, a portion of the moat.

Llanmaes
(Malefa(u)nt, or Malifant Castle)

Remains of walling
Location: Just to the north-east of Llantwit Major (SS 982 694)
Access: Visible from minor road

Llanmaes can be reached via a minor road which heads north-east from the B4265 on the edge of Llantwit Major. Drive into the village, and park near the church. Walk along the road heading south-east away from the church and the remains can be seen behind Quarry House which you will soon reach on your left.

Even though CARN: the database of the Royal Commission on Ancient and Historic Sites in Wales, classifies Llanmaes Castle as a tower house, the slight remains are difficult to classify definitively.

Today, only a few lengths of wall survive, none to their full height, although they do feature a fine set of putlog holes. Archaeologists speculate that the structure dates to the 14th century and that it had two levels: a ground-floor basement and a first-floor hall and solar.

By the 12th century, a knight's fee existed at Llanmaes, which was then probably the property of the de Sully family. Quite possibly a ringwork originally stood here, but nothing survives of the earlier site to verify this presumption. In the early 14th century, ownership passed first to William de Braose by right of marriage and then to the Fleming family. By the century's end, the Malefants had acquired the fee and probably built the fortified structure/tower house. In 1488, the estates passed to Jasper Tudor, Duke of Bedford and Lord of Glamorgan. Upon his death in 1495, they reverted to the monarchy.

During the 16th century, Charles Somerset, Earl of Worcester, leased the Malefant lands, which then passed to William Herbert, the future Earl of Pembroke. Ultimately, the estate became the property of the Marquesses of Bute.

When standing at the driveway at Quarry House, scan the horizon at the rear of the open field across the road. A low mound is all that remains of what is believed to be a moated site called **Bedford Castle**, perhaps in honour of Jasper Tudor, Duke of Bedford. Even though the square-shaped site has been classified as a moated site, definitive proof of the existence of a moat has yet to be discovered. Located about 183 metres south-south-west of the church, Bedford Castle has been severely degraded by ploughing. When a survey was conducted in 1976, earthworks still enclosed the entire site and a low, stony mound occupied the western corner. Quite possibly, the small mound would have supported a dovecote rather than any residential tower.

The site of Bedford Castle

Llanquian
(Llancovian Castle)

You want to park near the café that stands on the minor road that leads to Aberthelin above the junction between the A4222 and A48 to the east of Cowbridge. It is best to reach this spot by travelling along the A4222 towards Cardiff, and turn right onto the minor road just as the A4222's slip road starts to descend to join the A48. You will almost immediately see the café on your left.

Take the gravelled track that also doubles as a footpath from where you have parked which initially parallels the A48 but presently turns left away from it. This leads straight to Hollybush farm. Whilst the footpath technically continues through the farmyard straight past the house, the owners prefer that you turn right and then left through the next gateway and walk alongside their horse arena, turning left at its end, and then right to pick up the line of the path. This then bears slightly left through more gates to soon pass the ringwork which is in a clump of trees to the immediate right of the path.

The oval ringwork has portions of the original enclosing ditch and drystone revetment still intact. Dating to the 12th century, the ringwork was probably the centre of a sub-lordship of the larger lordship held by the St. Quintins at Llanblethian.

Llanquian first appears in the historic record in 1262, when it was described as being held by Philip de Nerber of Castleton for ¼ of a knight's fee. The castle may have been destroyed by Owain Glyndwr during the Battle of Stalling Down (also known as the Battle of Llanquian) in 1400. However, the de Nerbers continued to hold Llanquian until the 16th century.

Llanquian's ringwork is well hidden underneath a stand of trees, whilst a fence cuts across the ringwork and bars further passage. However, one can explore most of the mass of earthen remains. At the north-west corner of the castle, remnants of a 13th-century rectangular tower or first-floor hall survive; they now only stand to basement level. The barrel-vaulted chamber can be identified by its springers, and portions of a mural staircase also remain. To the south, a square structure projects from the embankment; possibly dating to the 13th century, it may mark the site of the original entrance onto the ringwork.

Llantrisant

Substantial remains of stone ringwork
Location: Near the centre of the village, itself some 8 miles
north-west of Cardiff (ST 048 834)
Access: Freely accessible at any reasonable time

Llantrisant is best reached from the M4 by taking the A4119 at exit 34 and heading north to the B4595, which skirts the south side of the village. To reach the castle, drive up Swan Street, which runs along the right side of the town's central circle, and park near the church. Stroll up the road alongside the red letterbox to the left of the church. At the top of the hill, take the gravel-covered footpath which cuts to the left between the houses. At the path's end, the castle ruins pop into view, masonry to your right and the outer bailey to the left. An alternative route is to park in one of the free car parks in the town centre. Walk up the hill to the left of Model House, and turn left onto the lane pointing to the 'castle green'.

From afar, one can easily spot the ruins of Llantrisant Castle standing to the right of the parish church of the three saints – Illtyd, Gwynno, and Dyfodwg – who gave the town its name. However, when in the town centre, the ruins all but disappear behind tall buildings, homes and pubs. Situated near the Guildhall and other historic buildings in the midst of a scenic spot enclosed with an ironwork fence and maintained by the local council, Llantrisant Castle is an interesting ruin.

At one time a lordship castle, its origins are uncertain; however, documents record the presence of a castle in 1246, when Richard de Clare was Lord of Glamorgan (see Chapter III for more information on the de Clare legacy). More than likely, an earth and timber castle existed at Llantrisant prior to Richard de Clare's stone stronghold; however, the identity of its builder remains a mystery. Historians have long speculated that Earl Robert FitzRoy of Gloucester, the second Lord of Glamorgan, constructed the original castle. After defeating the combined forces of Hywel ap Maredudd, Welsh Lord of Meisgyn, and Richard Siward, Norman Lord of Llanblethian, Talyfan and Rhuthin, de Clare would have underscored his victory by refortifying the castle and establishing a medieval borough at Llantrisant. Strategically located between the minor lordships mentioned above, the site's position at the edge of the projecting spur gave occupants a panoramic view of the countryside.

Erected on top of an artificially modified outcrop of land underlain by Pennant sandstone, Llantrisant Castle looks more like a motte rather than a ringwork, its accepted classification. However, the survival of what appears to be a ring-bank enclosing the inner ward and a faceted curtain wall supports the notion that the first castle on the site was a ringwork, even though it is partially obscured by spoil from horticultural work piled up alongside the embankment.

At least two massive round towers guarded the interior: the keep, which faced the more vulnerable northern end of the castle, and a southern tower which overlooked the Vale of Glamorgan beyond the cliff's edge. In the 13th century, when round towers became fashionable, Richard de Clare strengthened Llantrisant Castle with a stone keep, which is presently obscured by ivy and may have replaced an earlier timber tower. Christened by Leland as the 'Raven Tower', and also known as 'Giguran' ('gigfran' means 'raven' in Welsh), the keep probably stood over 14 metres high and had walls over three metres thick. Today, about a quarter of the structure still rises to an imposing 13.2 metres. Even though thick masses of vegetation cover most of the masonry, the rubble core is visible near the base of the tower. Reputedly built on the site of the original ditch, which a new ditch subsequently replaced, the Raven Tower may have stood alongside the main gateway, which no longer survives. Of the southern tower, only a rounded stone projection pinpoints its location.

Adjoining the keep, the oblong, bracken-covered inner ward had a diameter of roughly 27.5 metres and was protected by a ditch and the faceted curtain wall. Fragments of the inner wall survive: two lengths still flank the eastern side and a third is exposed on the west. While most of the surrounding stone revetment was rebuilt in the 18th and 19th centuries, a short length of medieval masonry consisting of local Pennant sandstone can be distinguished near the centre of the western side. The large outer bailey defended the inland sides to the north and east of the keep and inner bailey.

In 1317, Hugh le Despenser became Lord of Glamorgan, much to most people's chagrin. Four years later, the barons rebelled against Despenser and destroyed Llantrisant and its castle. By 1326, though, Despenser had rebuilt the stronghold. The timing was critical, for shortly thereafter, Despenser and his king, Edward II, were on the run in Glamorgan. Captured nearby, the two men were imprisoned in Llantrisant Castle, where they stayed until being moved to England to await their fates.

During Thomas Despenser's minority from 1375 to 1394, the monarchy controlled and refortified Llantrisant Castle. The Lords of Glamorgan continued to hold the castle until Jasper Tudor's death in 1495. Afterwards, a series of constables held the structure for the Crown but, by the time of Leland's visit in 1536, it had fallen into ruin. Interestingly, Leland also recorded that the site was in use as a prison, so the keep must have been at least moderately sound at that time.

Other historic buildings of note in Llantrisant include the Guildhall; the 19th century Parish Offices, which now house the town council; Model House, the former workhouse; and the parish church, which dates at least to the 11th century. The sites of the Bull Ring and the Victorian water pump are also worth a look.

Llantrithyd

Eroded ringwork remains in a small, atmospheric settlement
Location: The small village is 4 miles east-south-east of
Cowbridge (ST 046 727)
Access: A public footpath passes the site

The site is worth visiting, not so much for its ringwork, but for its church and the remains of Llantrithyd Place, a 16th-century house. To reach the village, head east along the A48 from Cowbridge, take the third minor road right (at a crossroads) and shortly turn right again at a fork. Carry on along this road and you'll reach the village in about half a mile. Park above the church near the phone box. (The remains of Llantrithydd Place are to the south-west of the church)

To reach the ringwork, walk back along the road and take the little road to the right that drops downhill to the immediate east of the church. When this joins the next road, turn right and you'll shortly come to a public footpath signed off to the right just beyond the last house. Walk along this and the ringwork will appear above and to your right just past the end of the hedge line on your right.

Established in the early 12th century, Llantrithyd's modest ringwork probably functioned as the sub-fee of the de Cardiff family. Followers of Robert Fitzhamon, the de Cardiffs were granted the half knight's fee sometime before his death in 1107. Historical documents do not indicate the exact year the de Cardiffs acquired the castle. However, a small cache of silver coins found in the remains of an aisled hall during excavations in the 1960s dated the structure to between 1122 and 1124. Two of the coins were produced at Henry II's mint in Cardiff.

Best recognised from the eastern side, the low ditch and ringbank surround almost the entire site, which has a diameter of about 56 metres. Having been extensively quarried and in-filled, the western side of the ringwork is heavily worn down, and the northern side falls sharply to the trickling waters of the canalised Llantrithyd Brook. The brook runs through the village and still fills the Tudor fishponds north-west of the ringwork.

Archaeologists have excavated only about half of the earth and timber castle; the numerous turf-covered humps they left behind mark the position of medieval buildings on the ringwork's northern and eastern sides. The oldest of the buildings, a six-post timber structure, stood at the south of the site. It may have served as the original gatehouse, a granary, or a storage building.

On the opposite side of the ringwork, archaeologists identified three later structures, including an impressive ten-post, six-bay aisled hall partially built into the earthen embankment at the north-western edge of the ringwork. Surrounded by an unusual drystone wall with rounded interior corners, the hall measured 16 by 10m. Probably entered on the west from inside the ringwork, the building would have had a thatched roof. The cache of medieval coins mentioned above was found during the excavation of this structure.

An unusual circular building with a diameter of about 5 metres was also discovered during excavations. Probably erected at the same time as the aisled hall, this drystone walled building was embedded into the ramparts at the northern end of the site and opened into the interior of the ringwork. It evidently stood at the north-eastern corner of yet another ten-post, rectangular building. Because this timber-framed building was erected after the circular structure, how they are associated, if at all, remains unclear. The structure may have replaced the larger aisled hall mentioned above sometime after the 12th century. Alternatively, it may have served as an observation tower, kitchen, or dovecote.

In addition to the medieval buildings, archaeologists unearthed prehistoric and Roman artefacts, a variety of potsherds, including pieces of green-glazed (Ham Green) pottery, and some metalwork. Records from 1262 mention that William de Cardiff was responsible for Welsh tenants in 'Landrired' and support the notion that his family still occupied the ringwork. However, the same document may actually refer to Horseland Moat, which was established nearby in the early 13th century. The de Cardiff line died out in the 14th century when the last heiress married into the Basset family. By then, the moated site superseded the ringwork.

Llantrithyd Place can be seen by returning to the churchyard. Begun in the mid-16th century by John Thomas Basset, the grand manor house consisted of three main wings, which together formed a U-shaped structure and was built with Lias limestone obtained locally. John Basset was one of a series of distinguished personalities who lived at Llantrithyd Place. After heiress Elizabeth Basset married Anthony Mansel, son of Sir Rice Mansel of Margam, Llantrithyd Place passed to the Mansel family later in the 16th century. Anthony lavished attention on the mansion and was responsible for the network of fishponds. After Mary Mansel wed Thomas Aubrey, modifications, including the addition of elaborate plasterwork, were made to the manor house. Nevertheless, by the late 18th

Llantrithyd Place

century the Aubreys abandoned Llantrithyd Place in favour of their new estates at Boarstall, and the site was left to decay.

Today, Llantrithyd Place is extremely ruined and inaccessible. The central wing contained the hall and parlours on the ground floor and a long gallery and hall on the level above. The two side wings, which point away from the church on either end of the central block, flanked a large central courtyard and held more residential chambers. Of the three sections, the northern one is the best preserved, but all of the structures are basically beyond repair.

Just south of the main house, the remains of several outbuildings, including a barn and a dairy or cottage, also survive. The huge area immediately south and east of the manor house contains two walled terraces and a noteworthy set of rectangular fishponds. The manor's orchards once stood to the north of the house. Running in a straight line from the south-eastern corner of the manor house, a raised walkway, now distinguished by moss-covered stone blocks, extends to a water-rimmed viewing platform.

The **church of St. Illtyd** dates in part to the 14th century and stands on the site of an earlier Norman foundation. Notable features include two armorial plaques devoted to the Aubreys that once adorned the manor house; a 14th-century effigy; a slab inscribed with the name 'Robert de Rievaulx, Abbot of Margam, died 1307'; and several monuments dedicated to members of the Mansel, Basset, and Aubrey families.

Located about 600 metres south-west of the church, **Horseland Moat** consists of an extensive maze of earthworks. (There is no public access to this, but some of the earthworks can be espied from the road on from where you have parked, just before you enter the next small settlement of Tre-Aubrey. The earthworks lie on the far side of the brook which itself flows below the road on the left.) The 13th-century site is comprised of four distinct elements: a moated island and the foundations of a medieval structure, the moat (intact only on the east), a set of trenches to the south-east (possibly used for cultivation), and the 18th-century Horseland farmhouse to the west. Horseland Moat apparently served the administrative and residential needs of the manor until Llantrithyd Place was built in the 14th century.

Loughor

Substantial stone remains of a ringwork
Location: It sits prominently above the junction of A484
and A4240 to the south-west of Loughor, by the bridge across
the estuary (SS 564 979)
Access: Managed by Cadw and freely accessible
throughout the year

The castle is accessed off the A4240. Constructed on a promontory carved by glacial action, Loughor Castle watched over the western reaches of the lordship of Gower. The River Loughor (Afon Llwchwr) curves west at this point and flows farther southward to Burry Inlet and thence onward into Carmarthen Bay. Here, Roman soldiers from the Second Augustan Legion established an auxiliary fort, *Leucarum*, in about AD 75 to guard a major communications route that stretched from *Viroconium* (modern Wroxeter in Shropshire) to *Moridunum* (Carmarthen). The road probably linked several forts and fortlets across southern Wales, including *Nidum* (Neath), which was only 15 miles east of *Leucarum*. Essentially rectangular in design, much of the Roman site at Loughor has been destroyed or buried underneath later construction.

The Roman fort's location was finally pinpointed in 1969 during excavation of the castle site. The dig revealed traces of the enclosing wall and pieces of Roman-era pottery. Evidently, the Romans abandoned *Leucarum* in the mid-2nd century AD, but reoccupied it briefly from the late 3rd to early 4th centuries before leaving it permanently.

In about 1107, Henry de Beaumont, 1st Earl of Warwick, became Lord of Gower and granted Loughor (and nearby Talybont) to his steward, Henry de Villers (also known as Villiers or Viliers). De Villers probably began the ringwork castle at Loughor shortly thereafter, but he remained in the area only until de Beaumont's death in 1119. The castle consisted of an oval mound, with the highest edge reinforced by an earthen bank. The embankment originally stood only two metres high and would have been fortified with timber ramparts, which no longer survive. Archaeologists have identified traces of the timber kitchen and bake oven that once stood inside the ringwork.

Although no longer in residence, Henry de Villers kept possession of Loughor Castle. In 1119, Henry de Neubourg, son of the 2nd Earl of Warwick, managed the property for his mother, Countess Margaret. In 1151, the Welsh rose up against de Neubourg, attacking Loughor Castle and probably burning its vulnerable timber defences. Scorched Norman chess pieces and gaming counters, bone plaques, and carbonised unspun flax discovered during excavations may date to this event.

After the fire, Henry de Neubourg seized Loughor Castle from Henry de Villers and held it until 1166, when the rightful owner, William, 3rd Earl of Warwick, took possession. More than likely, de Neubourg rebuilt the castle, widening the encircling embankment and erecting a stone building, possibly a tower, in addition to new timber structures. Notable finds from this period include strips of gilded bronze, used to decorate wood or leather.

Over time, successive owners strengthened the castle's defences in response to the continued threat of attack by the Welsh. During the early 13th century, the castle passed to the de Braose family. Despite arranged marriages intended to keep the peace, the Welsh continued to rebel against the Normans. In 1215, Rhys ap Gruffydd briefly held Loughor Castle, and others in the area, but, in 1220, John de Braose managed to regain custody of the castle. De Braose added a low stone curtain wall, of which only the foundations survive, and then left the castle to his heirs, William de Braose II and William de Braose III, who completed its construction.

In 1302, William de Braose III granted control of Loughor Castle to his steward, John Iweyn, who probably built the two-storey rectangular stone tower, which still stands, albeit in ruin, on the western side of the ringwork. Fireplaces, decorated windows, and a garderobe suggest that the tower was residential, although its cramped quarters would have offered little except the most basic comforts. The main gateway stood next to this tower; nothing of note survives. Speculation exists that a second tower was erected at a later date.

Ultimately, Loughor Castle never developed into a major fortress. What survives today consists of a mound surrounded on two sides by a steep-sided terrace, which traces the site of the medieval defensive ditch. The severely sloping sides of the site, which may more accurately be classified a ring-motte, rise to a level platform, where bumps of earth indicate the presence of foundations. To the west, the ruined tower protrudes over the side of the mound. The builders embedded the structure into the ditch in order to free up as much space as possible in the already confined ringwork. Three of the four walls of the plain brown tower, which was built with Pennant sandstone, still stand. The fourth has toppled onto its side and leans to the south-east. It contains fragments of a spiral staircase.

By the end of the 14th century Loughor Castle as an active site had largely disappeared from the historical record. In the 16th century it was documented as a ruin. The castle was neglected until 1948, when the State took over its care and consolidated the site.

Morganstown

A motte
Location: On the northern edge of Morganstown, itself near the
junction of the A470 to Merthyr Tydfil and the M4 (ST 128 819)
Access: Visible from the nearby road and car parks

Take the M4 to exit 32 and then go north on the A470. Continue to
the next exit, signposted for Tongwynlais, and turn onto the B4262,
heading south towards Radyr. Watch for the Tynant Inn which
you soon reach. Park nearby and walk back to cross the roadway.
The motte is visible at the road's edge near the traffic lights, but
is best accessed from the garden centre. Walk south just past the
Morganstown Rugby Football Club. The motte is located in the
trees at the rear of the car park. Fine views of Castell Coch are
possible from the B4262 and also from atop the motte.

At one time, Morganstown Castle and Castell Coch functioned
together to control the winding Taff gorge just north of Cardiff.

The flat-topped mound still rises to a height of about 5½ metres.
Its partly tree-covered, grassy summit stretches about 36 metres
across. A water-filled ditch surrounds the western side, but has been
filled in on its northern and eastern sides, mainly with grass trim-
mings from the neighbouring garden centre.

Like so many mottes in Glamorgan, little information about
Morganstown Castle exists in the historical record. Historians
believe the motte was established by the early 12th century and
may have served as the manorial centre for Radyr (Radur), which
was part of the lordship of Meisgyn (Miskin).

135

Morgraig

Some stonework remains of a substantial enclosure castle
Location: 2 miles south of Caerphilly, adjacent to the A469
(ST 160 843)
Access: A questionable footpath leads off from a pub car park

Castell Morgraig is a one-of-a-kind castle in a one-of-a-kind location – immediately behind the Travellers Rest Inn, a thatched public house on the A469 a couple of miles south of Caerphilly at Thornhill. At the far end of the pub's car park there is a locked gate beside a semi-stile beyond which is a well trodden footpath, though this is not marked on OS maps as a definitive footpath. The castle lies just a few hundred yards along the ridge and its path.

Located at the southernmost edge of the Welsh commote of Senghennydd Is Caeach, the castle would have been well placed to watch over the surrounding area. From this spot, panoramic views once reached to Cardiff and, beyond, to the Bristol Channel. Despite the padlocked gate, the site can easily be accessed from this point.

The walk from the car park to 'the Castle of the Great Ridge' climbs quickly as it traces the ridge, known as Craig Llanisien. Stone from the ridge was quarried as building material for the castle.

Besides the chunks of quartz conglomerate, the medieval builders also used local limestone and sandstone; most of the windows were dressed with Sutton stone. A narrow gully cuts along the middle of the ridge, which is strewn with chunks of rubble. From 1903-1905, the Cardiff Naturalists Society excavated Castell Morgraig and dumped much of the rubble outside the northern walls. Masonry from the ruined keep and towers is also scattered throughout the interior of the castle. Humps and dips fill the grassy courtyard and make footing somewhat difficult.

Morgraig was a pentagonal enclosure castle guarded by four D-shaped angle towers or bastions. A fifth, rectangular tower probably functioned as the keep. The tallest of the towers, the keep stood at the east on the highest point of the ridge. Though it now only survives to foundation level, the keep once stood well above the rest of the castle. Its walls were about 3 metres thick.

The four smaller towers at Castell Morgraig projected outward well beyond the curtain wall, which was at least 2.4 metres thick. Even though the wall still rises to a height of about 4 metres, at one time it probably stood at least another metre higher. On the western side of the site, between two of the angle towers, a modest gateway opened into the castle. It still serves as the main entrance.

The south-western tower is the best preserved of the four. It retains its oval foundation, which evidently helped prevent the tower from collapsing at the point where it projected away from the curtain wall. The north-eastern tower is believed to have been the site of the kitchen. Recesses in the north and south walls probably held fireplaces, and a small recess at the northern side of the entrance once contained an oven. A rubble-filled, rectangular pit in the section of wall between the north-eastern tower and the keep served as a cesspit. A postern gate once opened to the south-east of the cesspit, but now it only consists of a gap in the curtain wall.

Even though most historians (and this author) favour the belief that Morgraig was a Welsh-built castle, the Royal Commission speculate that it may actually have been the work of Richard de Clare, who annexed the commote in 1245. The Commission state that, as Castell Morgraig stood on the northernmost fringe of the English-held lordship of Glamorgan, it may have functioned as a 'border stronghold' which would have been used a base for English cavalry units patrolling the boundary zone. The Royal Commission attribute the castle's construction to de Clare, largely because it is simpler in design than his son's castle at Caerphilly and because his other castles in Glamorgan were also fairly modest structures. However, whereas Richard de Clare's castles at Llantrisant and Talyfan were dominated by round keeps, Morgraig's was rectangular. This major inconsistency gives weight to the credible suggestion that the Welsh built Castell Morgraig.

The main reason why some characterise the site as Welsh-built is its unusual wheel-like layout, which was never duplicated at any English-built castle. However, there were also no other Welsh-built castles with a similar shape. But, like most Welsh-built castles, Morgraig is noteworthy for its isolated, ridge-top position and rectangular keep. It also had relatively weak defences and D-shaped towers, both of which are characteristics often associated with the castles of the Welsh princes.

Indeed, John G. Owen of the Caerphilly History Society observed that Morgraig has all the features of a North Welsh castle. He concluded that Gruffydd ap Rhys, Lord of Senghennydd, quite possibly built the castle for Llywelyn ap Gruffydd and modelled the keep at Morgraig on Llywelyn's keep at Dolwyddelan, in Gwynedd. The historical record says little about Castell Morgraig. Nonetheless, it seems plausible that Gruffydd ap Rhys began building Castell Morgraig in the 1260s to defend his territory from the de Clares. The castle was of little assistance to Gruffydd, for, in 1267, Gilbert de Clare II ousted the Welshman from his lordship and annexed the neighbouring Welsh uplands.

Castell Morgraig remained in sound enough condition in 1316 to play a role in the rebellion led by Llywelyn Bren. Rhun ap Gruffydd Fychan ap Grono, who probably held Morgraig during the uprising, may have been the castle's final tenant. By the 16th century, the unusual castle was in ruins. Other than the excavations and clearance in the early 20th century, no consolidation work has been done to the site. Sadly, the castle is rapidly decaying, and many of the features recorded by the Cardiff Naturalists Society have collapsed.

Morlais

A semi-basement room survives, along with pieces of walling
and much fallen stonework
Location: North-east of Merthyr Tydfil (SO 049096)
Access: Paths lead to the castle site, but can involve some steep
climbing

Park by houses on the road to the west of the site (the minor road that leads from the Heads of the Valley road (A465) at Dowlais to cross the Taf Fechan stream). At the Taf Fechan end of the line of houses a footpath leads on to the open hillside. Head directly up the hillside and the castle itself is perched immediately above a quarry.

Running along the crest of a narrow ridge of limestone, an elongated jumble of randomly strewn grey stones seems more like one of the local quarries than the ruins of a medieval castle. However, Morlais Castle is one of the region's most noteworthy monuments. The most substantial fortification was undertaken on the eastern side, the three other sides being fronted by natural, steeply sloping ground. The westernmost side of the castle has been disturbed by quarrying.

The devastation of the site belies its historical importance, for Morlais Castle played a key role in the fight between the Lord of Glamorgan and his neighbour, Humphrey de Bohun, Lord of Brecon, in the late 13th century. During the Middle Ages, the area covered the borderland between the two lordships. Probably thrown up by Gilbert de Clare II in about 1288, the diamond-shaped castle occupies the site of an earlier Iron Age fort. Overlooking the rivers Taf Fechan and Taf Fawr, which merge not too far away and flow into the River Taff, the location made an ideal vantage point. When de Clare began construction of this new frontier castle, he was well aware that he would incite de Bohun to the brink of battle; after all, the Lord of Brecon claimed the land as his.

The two men finally came to blows in 1290. King Edward I actively intervened to resolve the dispute and established a truce between the rival lords. Ignoring the truce, de Clare's men made several incursions into the lordship of Brecon, ravaging the countryside and killing several people. De Bohun, on the other hand, supposedly had accepted the terms of the king's order not to fight the men from Glamorgan, but he finally lost patience with the process (which Gilbert de Clare was blatantly ignoring) and sent his own men back into the fray in 1291. In January 1292, Edward I demanded both men appear at court at Abergavenny and promptly ordered their imprisonment in the Tower of London and the imposition of hefty fines. De Clare was ordered to pay 10,000 marks, whereas de Bohun received a lighter sentence of only 1,000 marks. The men were eventually freed from the Tower; the dispute was never really settled, but their attentions were diverted elsewhere. In 1294 or 1295, Madog ap Llywelyn led the Welsh against the Lord of Glamorgan and attacked Morlais Castle. Although the historical record does not specify what happened to the castle, more than likely it was destroyed, for nothing further is mentioned about the site.

Morlais Castle consisted of four main areas: the outer and inner baileys, formed with rock-cut ditches and embankments, were both located on the south side of the site beyond the curtain wall; a polygon-shaped outer, southern ward, several round towers, and the massive south keep were all inside the curtain wall; and the triangular inner, northern ward (also known as the inner court) dominated at the northernmost point next to a massive round tower which is often considered a second keep. The main entrance, which was through a gateway on the eastern side, gave access to the southern ward (also known as the outer court). A semicircular tower overlooked the entry from the north. A slightly smaller, rounded tower (sometimes known as the causeway tower) defended the curtain wall midway between the main entrance and the south keep, on the eastern side of the site.

The basement of the south keep

141

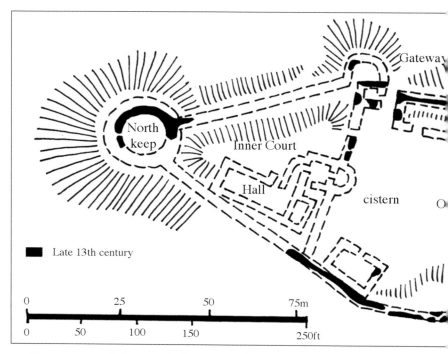

Late 13th century

| 0 | 25 | 50 | 75m |
| 0 | 50 | 100 | 150 | 250ft |

Fragments of the south keep are visible at the southernmost corner of the southern ward. Now capped with concrete to prevent further deterioration, only the basement level of the massive round tower survives to any significant degree. Accessible via a short set of steps, the remains include a 12-sided undercroft supported with dressed stone and ribbed vaulting and a well preserved central pier skilfully carved from local limestone.

Another round tower is barely identifiable alongside the south keep. Now little more than a gaping wound in the ridge-top, the south-western tower was reputedly larger and more impressive than the south keep. The western curtain wall may have extended northward from this tower; however, most of the wall is no longer retraceable. The ruins along the eastern curtain wall on the opposite side of the castle now consist of foundations and walling from a range of buildings that may have served as stables or accommodation.

Archaeologists have tentatively identified a squarish pit on the north side of the southern ward as a cistern. The 14-metre deep pit

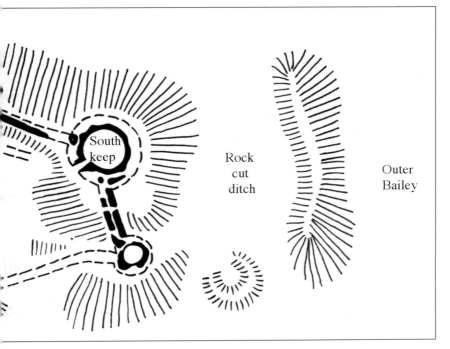

South keep

Rock cut ditch

Outer Bailey

is one of the castle's most curious features and may also have been used to impede unwanted access to the northern ward. Foundations of a square structure immediately behind the cistern may indicate the site of a kitchen or some other domestic building. A mound on the southern side of the cistern is a now dumping site for slag and spoils excavated during recent quarrying.

A small gap in the cross-wall on the north side of the southern ward provides access into the northern ward, originally the most important area in the castle. Today, foundations of the kitchen range, which contains a fine oven, and possibly either the great hall or a chapel survive along the southern and western sides. At the northernmost end of this area, a massive round tower – sometimes called the north keep – once dominated the entire site; in fact, it may have been larger than the great south keep. Archaeologists estimate that the north tower had a diameter of 18 metres and had walls some 3½ metres thick. On the other hand, the walls of the south keep probably were 5 metres thick but enclosed a basal diameter of only

9 metres. Like the south keep, the north tower was supported by a massive mound, but unlike the southern structure, most of the north tower projected beyond the flanking curtain walls. More than likely, the interior of both keeps were similar.

To the south of the masonry stronghold are the remains of two additional baileys which were fronted with ditches approximately 12 metres across and 4 metres deep. It is possible that the southern-most of the two baileys actually retains features from the Iron Age fort, but this notion has not been substantiated as rubble from the castle walls now fills much of ditch and makes it difficult to appre-ciate the original dimensions.

Mountyborough

A very overgrown earthwork remain
Location: Behind houses in the centre of Penrice in the Gower
(SS 492 879)
Access: No public access, but can be glimpsed from the 'green'
in front of the houses

Penrice lies on a very narrow minor road just north of Oxwich in the Gower. It is possible to park near the church on the 'Green' in order to obtain a glimpse of the very overgrown site directly behind Bay View and Sea View cottages which lie alongside the road.

Mountyborough ringwork dominates a glacial hill. Across the lane, the church of St. Andrew also tops the glacial ridge. Probably built at about the same time as the ringwork, the church retains its medieval tower, nave, and chancel arch.

Sections of the Norman ring-bank still survive on the south-eastern and south-western sides, enclosing an oval area measuring some 42 metres by 31 metres. The original entrance lies at the northern end. On the west, a deep ditch and counterscarp skirt the mound. In 1927, traces of two vertical timbers were discovered embedded in the embankment.

Even though there is speculation that Mountyborough ringwork was built by Henry de Beaumont in the late 11th century, more than likely it was actually constructed by members of the Penres family in the 12th century. The earth and timber stronghold probably served as the centre of the knight's fee until Robert de Penres replaced it with a substantial stone castle in about 1237. That castle, the largest on the Gower Peninsula, is located on the Penrice Estate, not too far to the north of the ringwork.

Neath

Substantial stonework remains
Location: Near the town centre and supermarket (SS 754 978)
Access: The gardens created from part of the site and gatehouse
are accessible from Monday to Saturday from 9am to 5pm, and
the perimeter of the site can also be walked

Head towards the town centre, the railway station and then Morrisons supermarket where you can park for a short while. In the 1990s, the local authority consolidated Neath Castle and landscaped the area in front of the gatehouse, and the gatehouse and gardens are open for exploration. Access to the inner bailey, however, is prohibited. Visitors can also walk the perimeter of the site; portions of the wall, however, are obscured by fencing and the Friend's Meeting House and burial ground, built in about 1799.

A stone sign marks the site of the Roman fort (*Nidum*) built in 75 AD to watch over the River Nedd (Neath) from its western bank. Now, a modern road, houses, and a large playing field cover the fort, the few remains of which lie scattered nearby. The location – the lowest fording point along the river – was ideal for observing activity along the waterway. Centuries later, the Normans also recognised the strategic properties of the spot, and, in the 1120s, Richard de Granville built a ringwork castle on the site. Though Granville's castle no longer survives, his more enduring project – Neath Abbey – remains one of the area's finest ruins.

In the mid-12th century, Robert FitzRoy, Earl of Gloucester and Lord of Glamorgan, established his own fortress, probably a ringwork, across the river on the eastern bank of the Nedd. Today, the plan of the ringwork is only reflected in the D-shape of the stone castle; most of the remains of Neath Castle date to the 13th century and afterwards. The river itself has long since moved away. FitzRoy's ringwork possibly acquired its stone defences in the late 1180s, after withstanding an onslaught by Morgan ap Caradog, Lord of Afan, who used siege engines to bombard the castle in 1184.

Almost 50 years later in 1231, Morgan Gam and Llywelyn ab Iorwerth destroyed much of the castle, which forced Richard de Clare, Lord of Glamorgan, to rebuild in stone. The castle was a fully operational stone fortress by the mid-13th century. In 1244, and also in 1258, the Welsh again attacked Neath. Now that the refortified castle had a strong curtain wall and two massive D-shaped towers guarded the northern corners facing the river, only the town suffered from the assault.

During Gilbert de Clare II's minority in the 1260s, Humphrey de Bohun, Earl of Hereford, managed Neath Castle and heavily garrisoned it against the Welsh. On 12 December 1282, that historic date when Llywelyn ap Gruffydd, the last Prince of Wales, was killed at Cilmeri (near Builth Wells), Edward I stayed overnight at the castle. After Gilbert de Clare III died in 1314, the Welsh renewed their assaults on Neath and other sites in South Wales. During Llywelyn Bren's attack in 1316, tower roofs and the curtain wall suffered significant damage. Once again, the castle was repaired and readied for battle, which next came in 1321, during the barons' rebellion against Edward II and his adviser, Hugh le Despenser, Lord of Glamorgan.

Hugh le Despenser soon began building the twin-towered gatehouse and equipped the gate passage with arrowslits, murder holes, and a portcullis. In 1326, he fled with Edward II to the newly strengthened castle, where the king reputedly stored some of his valuable treasure. Sadly, it has long since disappeared. Though now little more than a shell, Despenser's gatehouse stands its full two storeys. The older, northern tower was heightened and remodelled to complement the southern tower, which retains lancet-headed windows, corbels of Sutton stone, and a section of curtain wall from the original stone castle. Now facing the Friend's Meeting House, only traces survive of a square turret which once connected with the northern tower.

Despenser also built a new gate passage over the postern gate. Uncovered during excavations in the 1960s, the unique gate was located alongside a series of steps which led outside from the inner ward. Level with the flood plain of the River Nedd, the steps rose some 6.71 metres to the interior of the castle. The north-western tower stood on one side of the postern gate and the town walls on the opposite, southern side. The medieval drawbridge fittings survive underneath the modern wooden bridge.

Much of the curtain wall and the adjoining north-eastern tower now show their rubble filling, the dressed stone layer pilfered long ago. Jutting out from the curtain wall, the massive tower once stood as tall as the gatehouse. Now, it only rises a single storey above the basement, which was entered via a short set of steps. The large square turret immediately to the north once served as a garderobe tower; its lowest level held a cesspit.

Remnants of five separate structures, each fitted with cobbled hearths, line the interior wall between the north-eastern tower and the gatehouse. Historians are uncertain about each chamber's specific purpose. The one just south of the north-eastern tower, which has a round-backed hearth in one corner and what appears to be an oven in the opposite corner, probably served as the kitchen. The discovery of oyster shells, bone, and pottery fragments inside the structure supports this notion. Other buildings also lined the northern wall, but only traces survive.

During the mid-17th century, John Llewelyn leased Neath Castle, and later it passed to the Earls of Pembroke. In 1715, Charlotte Herbert, heiress to the Pembroke estate, sold the stronghold to its honorary constable, Sir Humphrey Mackworth, a leading magnate in the copper-smelting industry. Mackworth transformed Neath Castle into something of a playground and erected a large, round cockpit in the inner ward of which the foundations survive.

In recent years, houses, shops, and road works have encroached upon the castle. Walking through the neighbouring residential area, however, visitors can still identify the remains of the escarpment upon which the original castle once stood. A car park now covers the flood plain and also marks the edge of the castle property, where remnants of a revetted ditch are visible.

In the 1960s, the local authority made extensive repairs to the castle, whilst archaeological excavations were undertaken during the 1960s and 1970s. Today, the Neath-Port Talbot County Borough Council manages the site.

Newcastle Bridgend

Substantial stone remains
Location: Near St. Leonard's church, perched above the centre
of Bridgend which lies to the south (SS 902 801)
Access: In the care of Cadw and freely accessible
at reasonable times

The castle location is only haphazardly signposted in the town. At the roundabout junction of the A48 and A473 to the south-east of Bridgend, turn in to the town. Go straight over the first major junction, and then turn left, signposted for Porthcawl, at the next major junction. Take the first right (St. Leonard's Road) off the Porthcawl road near the first crest. At the T-junction turn right onto Well Road, and follow this round to the left. The castle sits above St. Leonard's church on the right hand side, and there is some parking provided.

Like its nearest neighbours, Ogmore and Coity Castles, the first castle at the site was probably a ringwork, which is mentioned in historical documents as having been built by Robert Fitzhamon in about 1106. Nothing remains of the ringwork, but the oval plan of the later masonry castle probably reflects its original plan. All three ringworks would have been positioned to guard the westernmost border of Fitzhamon's lordship.

By the latter half of the 12th century, the castle essentially consisted of a polygonal curtain wall, two square towers, and a simple, but quite decorative, gateway. More than likely, either Earl William FitzRobert of Gloucester, who held Glamorgan from 1147-1183, or King Henry II, his grandfather, added the stone defences. Henry II held the lordship from 1183 until his death in 1189.

In 1189, Isabel, FitzRobert's daughter and heiress, married the king's son, Count John of Mortain, who became king in his own right in 1199. Isabel actually lost possession of Newcastle Bridgend before their divorce in 1199, for John had granted the castle and lordship of Newcastle to his former enemy, Morgan ap Caradog, Lord of Afan. Morgan and his son, Leison, held the castle until Leison's death in 1213. Afterwards, Leison's brother, Morgan Gam, had expected to inherit the castle, but King John returned Newcastle to his ex-wife, Isabel. Isabel was then married to Geoffrey de Mandeville, Earl of Essex.

From the exterior, Newcastle Bridgend Castle's curtain wall appears to curve around the southern, western and northern sides; however, it actually consists of a series of short, straight sections of wall (facets). Buttressed by battered plinths, the walls were constructed with short, flat lengths of limestone rubble faced with

The Sutton stone carved doorway

Sutton stone ashlar. The straighter eastern side still tracks the top of the steeply sloping hillside.

The weakly defended main entrance, the drawbar holes for which survive, is adorned by Newcastle's finest feature – the carved, white Sutton stone archway, which is formed by two columns crowned with Ionic-style capitals. Sunken segmental panels and strips of pellets also decorate a recessed archway set above the main arch.

Positioned to defend the attractive but simple entry point, a square tower projected outward from the curtain wall just west of the archway. This three-storey high south tower probably held living quarters. Its basement level guard rooms still contain two tall fireplaces and Elizabethan-era windows. A set of stairs (now-blocked) situated inside the castle on the western side of the tower provided access at first-floor level.

Only foundations survive of the eastern range of buildings inside the bailey. Located closest to the curtain wall, the south-easternmost, rounded end of the range may mark the site of the now-vanished keep. (Alternatively, the keep may have stood on its own in the inner bailey.) The ruins immediately to the north contain traces of a central hearth. Across the inner ward from the eastern range, the empty shell of the west tower now rises only one storey. Originally, the tower may have provided accommodation. The only other masonry remains are the scanty foundations of the 'north building', the purpose of which is uncertain.

In 1217, Isabel (FitzRobert) de Mandeville died and Newcastle Bridgend Castle passed to Earl Richard de Clare by right of marriage to Isabel's sister, Amice. Shortly thereafter, Richard died and the lordship of Glamorgan and Newcastle passed to his son, Gilbert de Clare II. The castle was promptly turned over to Gilbert de Turberville, whose family had long been associated with nearby Coity Castle. Because the de Turbervilles focused most of their attention on Coity, little other than repair work was done at Newcastle. Believing himself to be the rightful heir, Morgan Gam did attempt to gain possession of Newcastle, but de Turberville had him imprisoned for a long enough period of time that controlling the castle became a non-issue.

In 1360, the castle passed to the Berkerolles family, and, after Sir Lawrence Berkerolles died childless in 1411, the Gamages claimed the stronghold and also neighbouring Coity Castle. In 1584, Barbara Gamage married Sir Robert Sydney, later Earl of Leicester, who then acquired the castle. Like their predecessors, the Sydneys neglected their Welsh castle in favour of their more prestigious holdings elsewhere in the realm and it began to decay.

In 1718, Samuel Edwin of Llanfihangel bought Newcastle Bridgend Castle and eventually it became part of the Dunraven estate. By 1833, the site had been transformed into a garden, which it remained until 1932, when it passed to the State, who consolidated the castle.

North Hill Tor

Possible ringwork
Location: On the north-west coast of Gower (SS 453 938)
Access: Public footpaths pass close to the site

From the church in Cheriton, on the north Gower, walk on the road uphill towards the coast. As the road swings right, take the footpath off to the left (in effect keeping straight ahead) and follow the lane to North Hill Farm. The path curves right and then left through the farmyard and then heads almost due north. The earthworks lie off the path to the left on the edge of woodland above mud flats.

Even though the ramparts on North Hill Tor resemble a partial ringwork, it seems more likely to this author that the site is actually an Iron Age promontory fort. However, because the Royal Commission classifies the site as a ringwork, it has been included in the gazetteer. However, only circumstantial evidence supports the notion that the site is medieval, for while the historical record clearly documents that the de Turbervilles occupied much of northern Gower, nothing exists to prove this site was a de Turberville residence. No doubt they owned the property, but that it served as any kind of castle remains debatable.

Regardless of its true nature, North Hill Tor is worth a visit, for the views of the surrounding landscape are unparalleled. Perched almost at land's end on the north-western tip of the Gower Peninsula, the craggy hillock overlooks Llanrhidian sands and marshy land immediately beneath the limestone cliffs, which once created an imposing natural barrier to invasion from the sea. The site consists of a strong partial embankment, ditch, and counterscarp, which swings around the south-eastern side of the promontory. A short stretch of drystone walling still supports the inner embankment, which once rose at least 7 metres. Unfortunately, the tor has been damaged by quarrying.

Norton Camp

Some earthwork remains
Location: Just to the north-west of Oxwich on the Gower
(SS 492 868)
Access: Can be seen, with difficulty, from a narrow minor road

About ¼ mile north-west of Oxwich Castle, the site lies between the farm buildings and woodland at Norton. The roadside hedge and bank obscures visibility, but the site is accessible with permission.

The builders of Norton Camp made shrewd use of the triangular layout of the site, which slopes naturally on all but the western side. An oval set of embankments marks the presence of a house platform in the north-western side of the ringwork.

The ringwork may have been constructed by the de la Mare family, who controlled the manor of Oxwich. Through various marriages the ringwork passed to the Penres family and then, in the 14th century, the Mansels acquired the property.

Ogmore

Substantial stone remains
Location: 3 miles south-west of Bridgend, by the River Ogmore
(SS 882 769)
Access: Managed by Cadw, the site is open freely
at any reasonable time

Take the B4524 south from Bridgend. At Ewenny, turn onto the B4524, and continue straight to Ogmore. The castle is signposted to the right.

Located immediately adjacent to the River Ewenny and only some 190 metres from the River Ogmore (Afon Ogwr), Ogmore Castle occupied a major fording spot into southern Wales. Placed on relatively flat land, though, the castle was not particularly well situated to guard the activity on the two rivers. However, the combined efforts of the castles at Newcastle Bridgend, Coity, and Ogmore, and the fortified manor at Candleston on the opposite side of the River Ogmore, ensured the vital communication route from the Bristol Channel was securely defended. Stories claim that King Arthur was born near the site and that the castle also marks the spot where the legendary hero was fatally wounded.

Ogmore Castle is a classic example of a ringwork refortified in stone soon afterwards. The earthen castle was begun by William de Londres, possibly as early as 1106. It must have been a substantial structure, for the massive earthworks still dominate the site. Originally, the oval-shaped, steeply banked earthworks enclosed an area measuring 50 metres by 35 metres. A deep, rock-cut ditch also surrounded the site; it was dry except during high tide, when the waters of the River Ewenny flowed inland. The inner ward would have held a variety of timber structures; timber ramparts originally offered moderate defence against attack.

Shortly after completing the ringwork, the Norman lord began converting the site into a stone castle. The castle's first masonry building was the simple square keep. Probably built by Maurice de Londres in the 1120s, the ruined keep is the castle's tallest surviving building. To reach the keep, one must pass through the extensively

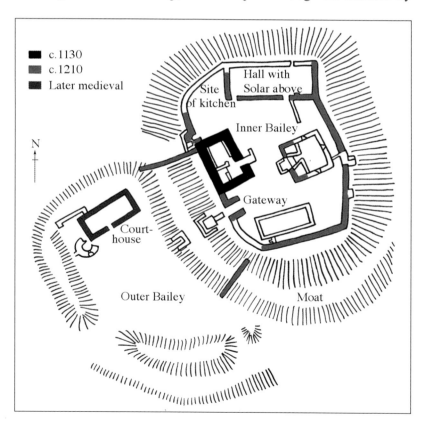

ruined gateway, a weak structure built during the castle's third building phase.

To the north of the archway, the remains of the two-storey keep still rise 12.5 metres. Only three of the four original walls survive, but they are substantial enough to indicate how the keep originally looked. Built with field stones and glacial pebbles interspersed with Lias limestone slabs, the structure was held together with brown mortar. Notable features include round-headed windows dressed with fine Sutton stone ashlar and an ornate fireplace, which would have been used to heat the first-floor great hall. Initially, the keep only stood one storey high; but, in the early 13th century another level with private apartments was erected, and a latrine tower was added to the exterior. Accessed from inside the keep, the well preserved two-storey tower contained garderobes on both levels.

Directly opposite the keep, the basement of what was once a freestanding square building, popularly known as 'the cellar', is situated below the main level of the inner ward. Accessed via three steps and a vaulted passageway, the unusual structure abuts the eastern bank of the ringwork, which can be reached by a different set of steps. A garderobe remains in the curtain wall at the far end of the cellar; window openings are all that survive of the upper levels. The building may have been used as living quarters or for storage.

During the early 13th century, builders added a simple hall with a central hearth to overlook the River Ewenny from the northern side of the inner ward. They also erected a postern gate, which opened to the outside at the south-eastern corner. Today, only foundations survive. Later in this same construction phase, another building was erected between the hall and the cellar; its new fireplace required the closure of the postern gate. Speculation exists that this structure may have served as the 'knighting chamber' mentioned in historical documents, rather than as the castle's hall. Foundations of another block of buildings, the purpose of which is unknown but tentatively identified as 'offices', are located close to the southern curtain wall.

The shell of a structure believed to be a courthouse stands in the outer bailey. Dating to the 14th century and rebuilt in the mid-15th century, it was actually the third building to occupy the spot. The roofless rectangular building has a simple doorway flanked by two large chambers. Remains of a 13th-century building are evident closer to the river, and a limekiln peeks out from beneath the southwestern angle of the courthouse. Builders apparently constructed the kiln on top of the 13th-century building and then added the courthouse over the end of the kiln. The structure, which may have contained the chapel, was used at least until 1631.

Ogmore Castle is first mentioned in historical records in 1116, when William de Londres abandoned it in anticipation of an assault by Gruffydd ap Rhys ap Tewdwr, who had already conquered the Gower Peninsula. Apparently the attack never occurred, and the castle remained a de Londres property for another century. After the death of Thomas de Londres in 1216, his widow, Hawise, married William de Braose, who held the castle from 1223 to 1234. After de Braose died, Hawise married Henry de Turberville, who died six years later. The widow's last husband, Patrick de Chaworth, lived until 1258. Their sons, Payn and Patrick, controlled Ogmore Castle for a time and then, in 1298, another de Chaworth descendant, Maud, inherited the site.

After Maud's marriage to Henry of Lancaster, her castle promptly transferred to the Duchy. When Henry became King Henry IV of England in 1399, Ogmore Castle then became a royal stronghold. The Welsh burned the castle during the Glyndwr rebellion in the early 15th century, and it probably remained derelict until the 1420s. Besides repairs, the limekiln and courthouse were evidently the only significant contributions to the castle made by the Dukes of Lancaster. In 1477, Edward IV granted the castle to his brother, Richard, Duke of Gloucester, but ownership reverted to the Crown in 1483. During that time, the castle's owners continued to make repairs, but, in the 17th century, it was documented as a ruin.

In 1928, the State became custodians of Ogmore Castle, consolidating and opening the site to the public.

Oldcastle Bridgend

A barn is believed to incorporate stonework from the castle
Location: Opposite St. Mary's church in Bridgend (SS 904 794)
Access: Parts of the barn are freely visible from a road

Situated on the other side of the road that serves St. Mary's parish church in Bridgend (on the other side of which is the A4063), a tithe barn, now merely a shell of its medieval self, overlooks a bend in the River Ogmore. Embedded in the north-facing wall of the barn are traces of a cross-oillet; on the western side, medieval mouldings and fragments of carved Sutton stone adorn a door. Sandstone quoins can also be detected. Historians believe these are the remains of Oldcastle Bridgend Castle.

Speculation exists that Oldcastle was probably replaced by Newcastle Bridgend Castle, the remains of which are located across the river less than a mile to the north-north-west. However, despite the names of the sites, the Royal Commission believe a reference to an Old Town mentioned in medieval documents in relationship to a lawsuit dealing with a knight's fee in Coity indicates that it is more likely that Coity Castle, which is only about two miles to the north-east, actually replaced Oldcastle.

Oldcastle-upon-Alun
(Castle-upon-Alun)

Two medieval doorways are all that remain
Location: In the centre of Castle-upon-Alun which lies 3 miles
due south of Bridgend (SS 911 748)
Access: One reused doorway is clearly visible

From Bridgend, take the B4265 south. At the far end of St. Brides Major, turn sharp left down a narrow lane signposted Castle-upon-Alun. Turn right at the T-junction you reach after about a mile. Ignore the turning immediately to the left and another soon after to the right, and you are 'in' Castle-upon-Alun when you reach the next road junction on the left.

The presumed castle site lies just north-east of this latter road junction, across the road from the farm of the same name. Two medieval doorways survive: one is embedded in a 19th-century boundary wall and the other in the barn alongside Oldcastle-upon-Alun House. Other early looking fragments of stonework appear to have been reused in the various buildings by the road junction.

Even though the Royal Commission hesitate to label the site at Oldcastle-upon-Alun as an actual castle, plenty of evidence strengthens claims that a castle of some significance stood here as early as the mid-12th century. While almost nothing survives to pinpoint the site, the village name, the defensive location (on the edge of an escarpment close to the River Alun), numerous references in the historical record, and the discovery of medieval potsherds and medieval masonry embedded in neighbouring buildings bolster the argument.

Oldcastle-upon-Alun was probably a freehold tenancy in the de Londres lordship of Ogmore. Payn of Oldcastle (Payn *Grossus*) occupied the site in the 1140s; his descendant, Peter of Oldcastle, served as the constable of Ogmore in the mid-13th century. Another descendant, Elanus (Alan) of Oldcastle, fought in the barons' rebellion against Hugh le Despenser in 1321. During the following two centuries, various tenants occupied the site, which was eventually replaced by new buildings.

Oxwich Castle

> Ruined 'mock fortified manor house'
> Location: On the south Gower coast (SN 498 863)
> Access: In the care of Cadw and open May to September for a fee

Take the A4118 west through Gower, and turn left at the sign for Oxwich. This road leads along Oxwich Bay and the up the far hillside to the site, which overlooks the bay. Technically, Oxwich Castle is not really a castle, but rather a 'mock fortified manor house' dating to the late medieval and Tudor eras in Wales. The extensively ruined site is included in this book for two reasons: it has several castellated features, and it stands on or near the site of two earlier medieval structures, either of which may have been the first Oxwich Castle.

Foundations of a rectangular tower stand shrouded in the woods on the headland to the north-east of the castle site. They indicate the presence of some sort of medieval fortification, perhaps a guard tower or a first-floor hall which may be the precursors to the present castle. Traces of a latrine turret stand at the north-west corner of the tower, the walls of which ranged between 1.1 and 1.5 metres in thickness. Less than a mile to the north-west, the considerable remains of an undocumented ringwork stand in the tiny hamlet of Norton. Even though they are probably the best candidate for Oxwich 'Old' Castle, we can only speculate that the owners abandoned Norton Camp in favour of the stone castle overlooking the bay.

Some documentary evidence survives in the historical record to suggest that a knight's fee existed at Oxwich as early as 1135,

161

and the Penres family may have owned the site as early as 1237, when it came to Robert de Penres by right of marriage to the heiress, Agnes de la Mare. However, it was another century before Oxwich (Oxenwich) Castle first appeared by name in the historic record. Then, John de Penres acquired the fee of Oxenwich, while the castle itself was granted to John's uncle, Richard de Penres, who also had control of Penrice Castle and fee and the fee of Port Eynon. In 1356, Richard, in turn, granted the castle to his son, Robert de Penres.

After Robert's death in the 1390s, Oxwich Castle and Robert's two fees at Penrice and Port Eynon passed to John de Penres' son, also called John, who already held the fee of Oxenwich. Shortly afterwards, in the early 15th century, Owain Glyndwr captured and imprisoned John de Penres II and seized all three fees and their associated strongholds. John remained a prisoner until 1408, when he regained the three Penres fees; two years later he died without an heir. His sister, Isabella, acquired John's possessions, which passed by right of marriage to her husband, Sir Hugh Mansel. In 1459, their grandson, Philip Mansel, was officially recorded as owner of Oxwich Castle. Except for a period of about 20 years (1464-1485), when King Edward IV confiscated Mansel lands due to Philip's support for the Lancastrian cause, the Mansels continued to own Oxwich and several other castles on the Gower until the 18th century.

Almost all of what survives at Oxwich dates to the massive rebuilding programme undertaken by Sir Rice Mansel and his son, Edward, in the mid to late 16th century. Only the recently discovered cross-wall in the east range predates this era, and may actually be medieval. Essentially, Oxwich Castle consists of two adjacent ranges of buildings surrounding a cobbled courtyard. The western half of the castle, which visitors encounter first, was constructed by Sir Rice during the first building phase at Oxwich; the eastern range was added later in the century by Sir Edward Mansel. At one time, the courtyard may have contained the castle gardens.

Sir Rice Mansel was a man with considerable influence in royal circles. Accomplished in battle, Rice not only served as chamberlain of Chester and was a member of the Council in the Marches, but was also a vice-admiral in charge of ten ships. He played an important role in Mary Tudor's coronation (his third wife, Cecily Dabridgecourt was one of Mary's best friends), and served as chamberlain of Carmarthenshire and Cardiganshire. For a time, Rice leased the property at Margam Abbey; but by 1540 he had acquired enough wealth that he could purchase the site outright. Sir Rice then converted the monastic buildings into a fine home, and, in 1580, Margam became the Mansel family's principal residence.

Modern-day Oxwich Castle seems small, its modest gatehouse stunted and fragile compared to the more substantial structures found at many medieval castles. While much of the curtain wall surrounding the inner courtyard has fallen, the enchanting gatehouse and south range reflect Rice's taste. Originally flanked on either side by solid round towers, the gatehouse is hallmarked by a fine heraldic emblem, which dominates the archway overhead. Added by Sir Rice in the 1520s and 1530s, the well-preserved emblem displays the Mansel coat-of-arms, along with those of the Scurlage and Penrice families, enclosed by Rice's initials and a circle of bay leaves.

Once through the main gate, visitors face an imposing wall pitted with several windows. A porchway once projected into the courtyard from this wall, but now only foundations survive. To the right, the south range of buildings now houses the ticket counter, gift shop, and exhibits. Until relatively recently, the range had been used as a farmhouse. If one looks past the displays, it is possible to identify remnants of Sir Rice's two-storeyed residence; for example, the fine fireplace and brick bake-oven prove that the room to the right of the entrance held the kitchen. More than likely, the room above, which also features a fireplace, contained the great hall; the smaller rooms to the right of the kitchen held the service rooms and servants' quarters. A short spiral staircase is housed in the round tower that stands between the south range and the gatehouse. Still accessible from the courtyard, the stairs take visitors to the wall-walk, which once passed over the gateway and around the curtain wall.

After Sir Rice turned his attention and finances to remodelling Margam Abbey, his son, Edward Mansel, continued to build at Oxwich. Well disguised behind the huge eastern wall, Edward's extensively ruined east range belies its Tudor grandeur. However, exploring the ruins, one can gain a real sense of the original magnificence of the place, particularly when standing at the base of the six-storied south-east tower. Originally, it was entered via the porch; nowadays, a gap in the wall allows access.

Shaped like a sideways 'E', Edward Mansel's 'great house' once had three enormous tower-like wings. Each projected outward from the high wall that formed the eastern side of the cobbled courtyard. Today, only the south-east wing stands to its full six stories; the middle wing has been levelled to foundations; and the north-east wing rises only partially. Interestingly, it still contains an impressive oven. A complex and confusing maze of stonework litters the central area of the east range. With some difficulty visitors can identify the ruins of the residential block, with its first-floor hall and fireplace, the long gallery overhead on the third storey, remnants of a pillar staircase, and vaulted basements. Windows with flanking seats puncture the western wall, which looks more like a skeleton than a home.

The south-east tower is arguably Oxwich Castle's most imposing structure. Despite having a massive splayed plinth to buttress the base, the tower seems poised to topple at any moment. Only when standing inside can visitors fully appreciate the building's unique character, which seems more like a modern-day skyscraper than a medieval castle. The sky-high walls are riddled with windows of varying height, and each single-chamber level had at least one fireplace. Quite possibly, this building and its siblings were built to house the Mansels' huge entourage of retainers and other workers. Gazing up to the skies, one can only feel awe.

A walk around Oxwich Castle would be incomplete without an examination of the ruined dovecote. Possibly built by Sir Rice Mansel, the building now lacks its dome and a large portion of its exterior wall. The gaping hole allows visitors to see the arrangement of the pigeon holes, which served as homes for doves and pigeons. The birds, in turn, were fed to the Lords of Oxwich during the harsh Gower winters. In its heyday, the dovecote held 300 pigeon holes.

By 1632, the Mansels had moved to their grander home at Margam and began leasing out Oxwich Castle. Allocated to a long series of tenants, the mock fortified manor house fell into disrepair, the east range decayed, and Sir Rice's south range became a working farmhouse. In 1949, Lady Apsley purchased the site and turned it over to the State to prevent its demolition. Since then, Oxwich Castle has been consolidated and is in the care of Cadw.

Oystermouth

Large stone castle
Location: Near the centre of the Mumbles, south-west
of Swansea (SS 613 883)
Access: Managed by the Friends of Oystermouth Castle,
it is open to the public for a fee during summer months.
The exterior is freely accessible throughout the year

Situated to overlook Swansea Bay, and now located just behind the row of shops on the northern side of the B4593 in Mumbles, Oystermouth Castle was probably begun by Henry de Beaumont, Earl of Warwick, who became Lord of Gower in about 1107. Control of the castle soon passed to William de Londres, who also owned Ogmore Castle and founded Ewenny Priory.

The unusual name, Oystermouth, translates from the Welsh *Ystum Llwynarth*. (The Welsh word, *llynarch*, means 'oyster'.) Over time, it has also been written as 'Ostrenuwe', 'Ostremew', 'Oystremuth', 'Oistremutha', and 'Oystremouth'. The shellfish was cultivated and gathered from the tidal sands which once flowed near the base of the castle. Historical records first refer to 'Oystermouth' in 1379.

The castle's oval plan and the minimal scarping done to the centre of the site support the notion that the original stronghold was probably a ringwork. The exact location of an associated bailey has been obscured over time, but it was probably just north of the castle in an area now camouflaged by trees. The open landscape around the other three sides of the site seems ample enough for an outer bailey; yet, no physical remains have been uncovered to support this theory. Indeed, the sloping hillside provided substantial natural defences; so, perhaps the castle's builders considered another bailey unnecessary.

More than likely, the Welsh assault in 1116 destroyed the earth and timber castle. (Some historians speculate that the site was actually refortified in 1136.) As a result, Maurice de Londres, William's son, decided to build a square stone keep atop the site. Situated almost directly opposite the gatehouse at the top of the slope, the remains of the once freestanding keep stand at the core of the castle. The keep, which measured 16.8 metres by 10 metres, was probably surrounded by timber defences until 1215, when Maelgwyn ap Rhys and Rhys Ieuanc stormed the Gower, burning the castle and several others on the peninsula. Today, only the basement level is relatively intact. It features a fine fireplace. Evidence of scorching may date to the Welsh attack of 1215.

Flanking walls and remnants of other buildings create the impression that the entire northern block, which includes the keep, formed a coherent complex. In reality, the mass of structures represents different building phases. One of the most impressive of the group, a small but substantial porch, stands at the keep's south-western corner. It was probably built as a replacement for the simple doorway (now blocked).

When owner Thomas de Londres died without an heir in about 1215, Oystermouth Castle passed to the lordship of Gower. Even though the castle disappears from the historical record for the next 40 years, it was probably controlled by John de Braose, who became Lord of Gower in 1220. De Braose extended the northern side of the keep, essentially doubling it in size.

In response to further assaults on the Gower in 1256 and 1288, William de Braose II again strengthened Oystermouth Castle. With the addition of a range of buildings north-west of the keep and another along the western wall, the castle was impressive enough that, in 1284, Edward I stayed for two nights. De Braose also heightened the curtain walls and the main gatehouse, arguably the castle's most striking feature.

Approaching from the town centre, the imposing sight of de Braose's gatehouse lures visitors to the castle. The simple structure originally rose two storeys high and was probably flanked by two semicircular towers, long since pulled down – or, perhaps, never completed. Murder holes, portcullis grooves, and drawbar holes were fitted in the gate passage. The gatehouse was probably converted to a residential building during the mid- to late-16th century.

As Lords of Gower, the de Braoses occupied Oystermouth Castle until 1321, when John de Mowbray, who controlled the stronghold by right of marriage to William de Braose's daughter, Alina, spearheaded a rebellion against the Crown. In response, Edward II granted the site to Hugh le Despenser, Lord of Glamorgan, in 1322. After the rebel barons were defeated at the Battle of Boroughbridge, John de Mowbray was taken to York and executed, and his wife and son, another John, were imprisoned in the Tower of London. Despenser abruptly swapped Oystermouth Castle, and others on the Gower, with Elizabeth de Burgh, the de Braose heiress, in exchange for the lordships of Caerleon, Usk, and Trelech. However, prior to handing the castles over to Lady de Burgh, Despenser ordered his own sheriff to plunder them.

In 1327, Alina de Mowbray reacquired Oystermouth Castle. She lived there for three years with her second husband, Richard de Peshale, whom she had met in the Tower of London. Tradition has it that Alina added the grand chapel block that dominates the inner ward immediately to the east of the keep. Constructed in the late 1320s or early 1330s, the stunning building still reaches its original three storeys. The rectilinear structure contained a basement, a first floor residential level, and a chapel on the uppermost level. Its square turrets projected into the inner ward. For a time, the basement served as a kitchen; it contains the remains of a fine fireplace. Though similar to the basement in plan, the first floor chamber contained more lavish furnishings, including a large, round-backed fireplace, a garderobe, and several ornate windows, which were once secured with shutters.

Lavish tracery windows rimmed with Sutton stone dressings and carved pieces brought from Neath Abbey adorn the chapel. The remains of an aumbry and piscina and vaulted recesses believed to be confessionals are embedded in the walls. Remnants of medieval painting also survive. Garderobes project outside the castle at the south-western angle, above the ruins of the kitchen block, and also near the modern ticket cabin.

After Alina de Mowbray died in 1331, the castle passed to her son, John. In 1354, Edward III appointed Thomas Beauchamp, Earl of Warwick, as Lord of Gower. Beauchamp spent little time at Oystermouth Castle, preferring his larger estates, such as Warwick Castle.

After Thomas Beauchamp II fell out of favour with his king, the Mowbrays regained control of the castle in 1397. Thomas Mowbray held Oystermouth Castle during the Glyndwr rebellion in the early 15th century, but neglected its maintenance. It is unclear whether or not the Welsh actually seized Oystermouth Castle.

In 1451, Sir Hugh Johnys became the castle's constable. During the 16th century, the Somersets, Earls of Worcester, became Lords of Gower and gained possession of the castle. Eventually, Edward, Marquess of Worcester, reacquired the decaying stronghold from Oliver Cromwell, who had held the castle for 16 years. Worcester's heir, Henry, became Duke of Beaufort, and the Beauforts retained Oystermouth Castle until 1927, when they sold it to the local authority in Swansea. Since 1927, Swansea has further consolidated the marvellous castle in Mumbles.

Pancross

> Low earthwork remains of a ringwork
> Location: 4 miles west of Barry (ST 047 700)
> Access: A public footpath runs alongside the path

Take either of the minor roads to Pancross from the B4265 north-west of Cardiff airport. At the crossroads in Pancross head north-west to the immediately adjacent hamlet of Crosstown. Just beyond the farm you quickly reach on the right hand side, and just before the buildings a bit further along on the left hand side, an unsign-posted public footpath leads off to the right (it is signposted from its other end, but that's a longer walk!). Take this footpath (which is to the south of a hedgeline, but crosses towards it) and you'll soon reach the earthwork remains close to the hedge and a field gateway, near the crest of the gentle slopes.

Sometimes known as Middlecross, the 12th-century ringwork and bailey castle near Pancross, Llancarfan, was only discovered in the 1970s. The site has been extensively carved up, used as fill for the adjacent hedgerows, and degraded by ploughing. Not surpris-ingly, the medieval castle is in poor condition. Fragments of the ringwork lay east of the outer embankment of the associated bailey, the earthen ramparts of which only survive on the westernmost side. A hedgerow separates the ringwork from the bailey.

Historians speculate that the site was named for an unknown Norman named Payn, who may have been a subtenant of the Umfraville lords of nearby Penmark.

169

Penlle'r

Earthwork remains together with slumped remains of stonework
Location: 3 miles south of Ammanford (SN 665 096)
Access: On open ground close to a minor road

Castell Penlle'r is best reached from Ammanford, by taking the minor road leading over the River Amman and east-south-east towards Betws and thence up the hillside beyond. The road crosses a cattle grid in about 1½ miles, and carry on and park where the road swings to the right. Then, walk to the summit of the hilltop ahead where, despite its mountain-top setting, Castell Penlle'r is visible for some distance and easy to identify.

Located at the northernmost edge of the Gower, adjacent to the former Welsh-held lordship, Is Cennen, Castell Penlle'r (which means 'high place of the castle') is one of Glamorgan's most unique sites. Perched some 374 metres high on the summit of Mynydd y Betws, the frontier castle was positioned to act as an early warning system to report attackers approaching from the north.

Even though the site's unusual, keyhole shape resembles a motte and bailey, historians believe Penlle'r probably dates to the 13th century, late in the history of motte castle building. More than likely, only a garrison lived at the castle for any length of time, and the peculiar design may have been well suited to a site intended merely for brief occupation. It was never used as a lord's residence. Alternatively, some historians think the unusual design suggests that the site was a native Welsh fortification.

As with so many castles in Glamorgan, the history of Castell Penlle'r is scanty at best. Most of what is known of the site has been determined by interpreting the historical record rather than from any physical evidence. Apparently, the castle may equate to 'New Castle of Gower' (*Novum Castrum de Gower*), which was held by William de Braose II, destroyed by Rhys Fychan in 1252, and may have been an earth and timber structure. After 1252, it would have been refortified with stone. Now, only fragments survive. Sadly, no other documents provide insight into the site, and it was probably abandoned in the 14th century.

Even though most of the rugged site is covered with bracken, the overall plan can be traced. Superficially, Penlle'r looks like a motte and bailey castle, with the motte section standing to the south and the larger bailey area to the north. The two parts of the site are separated by a deep cross-ditch, which measures approximately 76 metres by 45 metres along the north and 76 metres by 37 metres on the south and contains traces of what may be the footings of a bridge.

Both parts of the site contain remnants of stone structures largely hidden beneath several humps and bumps. Some researchers label these buildings 'huts' to indicate a temporary purpose, whereas others more confidently claim they were towers. The larger, square structure to the north may have functioned as an observation tower, and the smaller one may have been a keep. An impressive V-shaped ditch enclosed the entire site. Sections of counterscarp mainly on the southern side have slumped inward, which may indicate that the site was quarried or never completed.

Penllyn

Some stonework remains of the keep, adjacent to a later house
Location: 1 mile north-west of Cowbridge (SS 979 761)
Access: On private land, but can be glimpsed (at least in winter)
from a footpath which runs below the site

Head out of Cowbridge on the A48 towards Bridgend, and take the first right, and then the first right again. You want to park when this road starts to descend, and where another road meets it from the left. Walk through the gates opposite this road junction along the wide track which heads straight towards the castle, and then curves left to drop down below the ruins and then the house. The remains of the keep are on the near side of the range of buildings as you approach them.

The remains of the great keep still dominate the limestone ridge upon which it was built in the 12th century as the caput of the lordship of Penllyn. The Norris family held the castle until about 1400, when the last male heir died. After the castle passed to Lucy Norris, one of the four heiresses to the estate, Tomkin Turberville, her husband, acquired ownership by right of marriage. In 1535,

Watkin Lougher led a contingent of some 100 men and torched the castle; however, Christopher Turberville (Lougher's father-in-law) survived the attack and continued to occupy the castle. Shortly thereafter, they erected a manor house over much of the castle site, but managed to preserve the great keep.

In 1703, the Turbervilles sold the manor house and castle to the Seys family, who in turn sold the site to Sir Edward Stradling (of St. Donats Castle). Although Penllyn Castle was inherited by Miss Emilia Gwinnet in 1789, it was already a documented ruin. In 1846, John Homfray replaced Emilia's then newly built home with the castellated residence that is still occupied.

Only the north and eastern walls of the rectangular keep survive to any great extent; they still stand 8.5 metres high and were about 1.7 metres thick. The northern wall retains herringbone masonry. Accessed through a forebuilding, the keep probably held a ground-floor basement and a first-floor residential chamber.

Penmaen

Remains of a ringwork are clearly visible
Location: Half a mile south-east of Penmaen village on the southern Gower coast (SS 534 882)
Access: Freely accessible by a variety of paths

The question of reaching Penmaen depends really upon where you are able to park and thus your starting point. If you manage to park in Penmaen (on the north side of the A4118; there is no parking along the roads to its south), you can walk over the A road by the bus shelter onto the minor road, and then bear right when it splits. Past the last house on the right, when the tarmac has already give way to stone and gravel, a footpath points down the slope to the right, and if you follow this and then take one of the paths up the opposite slope once over the stream, the ringwork is very clearly visible on the first promontory of this hill. (If you look back up the inlet, you'll see the remains of Pennard Castle on the skyline. This can be reached across the stepping stones across the Pennard Pill – at low tide.)

One of the Gower's finest surviving ringwork castles guards the cliff edge overlooking the western side of Pennard Pill. Like

Pennard Castle, its neighbour on the opposite hilltop, medieval Penmaen has been almost completely encroached upon by sands shifting over the course of time. Fortunately, it appears that only a small portion of the castle has slumped down the hill towards Three Cliffs Bay.

When approaching the site from the north, the castle's earthworks gradually appear in the distance. An almost complete oval, the medieval ringwork was entered via a causeway that crossed a deep rock-cut ditch on the north-western side. A square timber gate tower once stood atop the ramparts at this point; traces were uncovered during archaeological excavations in the 1960s. Along the northern side of the inner ward, archaeologists also discovered remnants of two small square structures.

After a fire destroyed the gate tower, probably in the late 12th century, the owners filled in the entranceway, heightened the north-western embankment, and refortified Penmaen Castle in stone. The exterior ditch was also deepened. Inside the castle, a round-cornered stone structure was added to the southern side which probably served as the hall.

According to historical documents, during the 13th century Penmaen was supposed to have been restored to Philip Hareng. Hareng's ancestors had occupied the area for some time and may have built the original stronghold in the 12th century. The Welsh, led by Rhys Gryg, destroyed the castle in 1217, and the Harengs were forced to flee and never re-occupied the site. However, they continued to own the castle until the mid-14th century, when the Blancagnel family acquired the castle as part of the fee of Penmaen.

Penmark

Several upstanding walls remain
Location: Behind the church in Penmark, itself 4 miles west of
Barry (ST 059 689)
Access: On private ground, but can be seen at short a distance
from the churchyard, most readily in winter

The ruins of medieval Penmark Castle are located amongst ivy and
some trees in a field at the rear of St. Mary's church in Penmark,
reached by signposted roads heading north off the B4265. To pay
a close visit, be sure to obtain prior permission from the owners of
Penmark Farm, opposite the church.

Composed of an inner and outer ward, the site combines traces
of an early 12th-century ringwork with stone buildings added in the
following century. Established by Robert Fitzhamon as a primary
caput for the region, Penmark Castle was constructed by the de
Umfravilles, Lords of Penmark, at about the time of Fitzhamon's
death in 1107. The compact castle sits on the edge of a steep scarp
which overlooks the River Waycock some 85 metres below.

The de Umfravilles owned Penmark Castle for over two centuries, and it then passed to the St. John family when Elizabeth de
Umfraville married Alexander St. John. The St. Johns continued

to hold the stronghold until 1656, when they sold it, along with their castle at nearby Fonmon, to Colonel Philip Jones, a leading Parliamentarian. By the 15th century, the Joneses had turned their sights to life in their finer castle at Fonmon and allowed the castle at Penmark to decline. Some historians have claimed that Owain Glyndwr assaulted the castle in 1402, but medieval records do not support this notion.

The earliest embankments can be identified in the layout of the oval inner ward and the walling which probably follows the perimeter of the ringwork. Penmark would have been one of Glamorgan's five largest ringwork castles, even surpassing Coity and Ogmore. Today, it barely reflects that status. Much of the castle is obscured by bracken and ivy, notably on the east and south-east sides where grass-covered ridges suggest the lines of medieval foundations.

The castle's dominant feature is the D-shaped tower at the north-west corner of the inner ward and which overlooks the valley below. Despite the undergrowth, the round-ended tower is accessible. It originally stood two storeys high and had narrow, splayed windows, one with seats and the other linking to the garderobe tower next door. The garderobe protrudes into the outer ward, and once also provided access to the wall-walk. A tall square tower faces outward on the western side of the tower. On the other side a section of the curtain wall stretches south-south-east from the latrine block towards the site of the main gate, which no longer survives. The wall still rises 5 metres and has traces of wall-walk. A length of curtain wall also runs south from the D-shaped tower along the line of the original enclosing ditch, which is now mostly in-filled.

A crumbling building, which once served as a dovecote, occupies the north-western corner of the outer ward. A long earthen embankment marks the ward's outer perimeter. During the Middle Ages, the earthwork would have extended to the churchyard.

During the mid-16th century, Penmark Castle was leased by tenants who adapted it for agricultural purposes. According to Iolo Morgannwg, the barn in the inner ward was built in the 18th century and most of the dovecote torn down (for building material?). Since then, little has been done to the castle to protect it from further decay. Descendants of the Jones family still own both Fonmon and Penmark castles.

Pennard

Substantial stonework remains
Location: Between Penmaen and Southgate on the south Gower coast (SS 545 885)
Access: Readily reached by a range of footpaths

The question of reaching Pennard Castle depends really upon where you are able to park and thus your starting point. However, a great way to approach it is from Penmaen, crossing the Pennard Pill by stepping stones (although not at high tide!), when the castle makes a memorable sight against the sky. If you manage to park in Penmaen (on the north side of the A4118; there is no parking along the roads to its south), you can walk over the A road by the bus shelter onto the minor road, and then bear right when it splits. Past the last house on the right, when the tarmac has already give way to stone and gravel, a footpath points down the slope straight ahead. Follow this and then cross the stepping stones. As you do so, the castle is clearly visible on the skyline to your left, and you can pick up one of many paths to reach it. (You may also chose to visit Pennard Castle; see the site entry.)

Perched on the very edge of a cliff overlooking Pennard Pill as it heads toward Three Cliffs Bay, crumbling Pennard Castle teeters on the brink of destruction, enduring the ravages of swift winds and blowing sands but with the aid of concrete buttressing. Acquired by Henry de Beaumont, 1st Earl of Warwick, as part of his conquest of the Gower Peninsula in the early 12th century, the earliest castle was a partial ringwork, one side formed by the natural slope of the cliffs and its inland front ditched. During the late 13th and early 14th centuries, the de Braoses, Lords of Gower, held Pennard Castle, and were responsible for most of the masonry refortification of the site. Today, only the plan of the ringwork survives in the layout of the later castle. However, excavations in 1961 revealed that the southern curtain wall was actually built into the earlier earthen embankment.

From afar, Pennard Castle exudes an air of impregnability. The twin-towered gatehouse (which apparently was modelled on Edward I's great fortresses in North Wales) is the castle's finest feature. However, even with all its Edwardian inspiration, the gatehouse was a flimsy building, and it now largely stands with the support of thick, modern concrete. The short gate passage was poorly defended with double doors, a portcullis, which dropped only part way to the ground, and a single arrowslit in the north tower. Basement levels of both towers contained guardrooms which were accessible from

the inner ward. Two curious features – square slots running at an angle into the gate passage from inside the guardrooms – may have been associated with a now-vanished drawbridge. Only a portion of the rear wall of the north tower survives; it once enclosed the interior chambers. The south tower retains pieces of the battlements.

Around the rest of the castle, the eroding sands have caused extensive destruction, and only one chunk of upstanding masonry remains. Portions of the 1-metre thick curtain wall still rise to wall-walk level on the northern side. At the north-western end, a square residential tower projects onto the cliff edge alongside a smaller round tower and a garderobe.

Just south of the two towers at the western side of the castle, fragments of a freestanding rectangular hall are still visible inside the inner bailey. The structure replaced an earlier timber hall, evidence for which archaeologists identified after uncovering charcoal and burned daub underneath the stonework. A type of building relatively common at ringwork castles, this particular structure actually predated the addition of the stone defences. It had three chambers, the central one of which would have contained the hall. The southernmost room was probably used as the solar.

In the early 14th century, the sand began to encroach upon the castle and its neighbouring village, which was abandoned in about 1532. Today, the scanty remains of St. Mary's church, which protrude from the dunes on the golf course side of the castle, provide the only physical evidence that the medieval village did exist. As at Kenfig Castle, a replacement church was constructed farther inland and St. Mary's was abandoned. The new church formed the focal point of the village that soon grew up around it.

Presently in the care of local authority, Pennard Castle seems poised for an imminent tumble. In fact, some parts of the small castle have slipped onto the valley floor far below.

Penrice

Substantial stonework remains of Gower's largest medieval castle
Location: Just south of the A4118 between Reynoldston and Penmaen on the Gower (SS 497 885)
Access: A public footpath passes below the site (from which the photograph on p.159 is taken), but the remains themselves are off limits

Take the A4118 west from Parkmill through Penmaen and past the turning left to Oxwich. Take the next narrow road left signposted to Penrice, and drop down to the valley bottom where there is a small car park on the right. A footpath leads off from the other side of the road from this car park over a stone stile and up a tarmacced drive towards the later Penrice Castle. The ruins of the earlier structure are on the rocky eminence above and to its left. The owners insist that visitors stay to the public footpath and walk past but not into the castle, which is inaccessible for safety reasons.

At the junction of the A4118 and a minor road leading south towards Oxwich Bay, travellers to the southern Gower Peninsula will find themselves confronted with what appear to be the remains of a medieval curtain wall. The towered ruins seem authentic enough, particularly since they flank the main entry point onto the Penrice Estate, long the site of a fine castle. However, the reddish-brown walls actually date to 1793, when Thomas Mansel Talbot lived at Penrice. Talbot is also responsible for the construction of Penrice Castle House, a plain 18th-century house designed by Anthony Keck. But it is the hulking medieval castle, the Gower's largest, that is the more remarkable site.

Located in the midst of lush woodland, high on a craggy hill that overlooks the historic estate, the impressive enclosure castle dates to the 13th century, when Robert de Penres and his family controlled most of the region. Over time, ownership passed to the Talbots, and, eventually, the estate became the property of the Methuen-Campbells, who still live in Penrice House at the foot of the medieval castle.

Although originating in Devon, the de Penres family took their name from the Penrice ('pen-rhys') fee on the Gower, which was in existence by the early 12th century. One knight's service was owed to the Lord of Gower for this fee. For the next two centuries, the de Penres heirs continued to hold the castle and surrounding estates, and also extended their holdings to include Oxwich Castle and other lands on the Gower. Robert de Penres (II?), who probably built much of the stone castle between 1237 and 1282, moved the family's caput about half a mile uphill from the large ringwork, Mountyborough, to the more powerful, naturally defended site. (The possibility exists that were two Roberts, perhaps father and son, who lived at Penrice during this period and that both oversaw the construction of the masonry castle.)

The new castle stood atop a vast outcrop of limestone which also made a convenient quarry for building stone. It consisted of the curtain wall, which enclosed an area measuring 97.5 metres by 70.1 metres and traced the line of the D-shaped headland on which it was perched. A round keep dominated the western side of the castle, which was more heavily fortified than the rest of the site, for the sharply-sloped south and eastern sides were formidable natural obstacles to an assault. Solid bastions were placed at several points along the perimeter and a simple gateway stood on the northern side (fragments survive inside the later gatehouse). Presently, only the exteriors of the bastions along the southern curtain wall are viewable. The western and northern sides are off-limits and, consequently, away from public scrutiny.

The completed castle featured a three-towered gatehouse, which was erected over the original gateway, and a large hall block, its three projecting towers constructed atop a portion of the earlier curtain wall. The interior was notably devoid of structures, except for the chemise on the eastern side of the keep and a large rectangular building, possibly a barn, situated along the eastern curtain wall. Minor modifications, including the addition of an internal porchway, were made in the 16th century. A circular dovecote was erected at the south-eastern corner of the wall. Projecting outward over the cliffside, it is visible to the public.

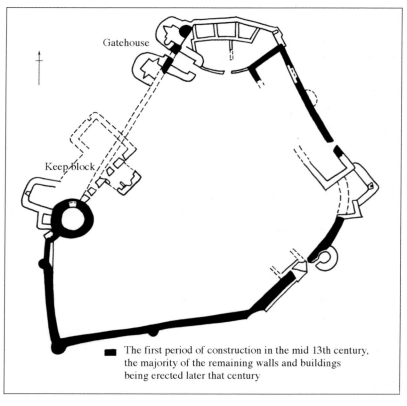

Gatehouse

Keep block

■ The first period of construction in the mid 13th century, the majority of the remaining walls and buildings being erected later that century

The original round keep had two storeys and stood just over 10 metres high. The basal diameter measured about 10 metres. Even though it lacked permanent staircases and fireplaces, the great tower did contain a small latrine turret on the first floor. During the latter half of the 13th century, a battlemented upper storey was added to the keep. This alteration probably occurred at the same time as the construction of the hall block.

During the late 13th century, the building projects were largely devoted to the main gatehouse and the hall block, the construction of which required the demolition of the north-western curtain wall. The two-storey gatehouse had two massive projecting square towers, each of which featured rounded external angles and square inner chambers. An internal tower with rounded angles and a square interior design was also erected between the two outer towers. Facing into the castle, it may have served as a 'gate-hall'. The gatehouse was defended by arrowslits, a portcullis, the grooves of which survive, and a set of timber doors. The narrow windows on the first floor, where the windlass room was located, were secured by draw-bars and shutters. The chamber also contained a fine round-backed fireplace and opened to passageways which linked the three towers. The two outward-projecting towers contained recessed windows with side benches, arched doorways, and fireplaces; traces of medi-eval lime plasterwork survive. A single latrine turret stood at the northernmost corner of the northern tower, near the curtain wall.

William de Penres probably added the unusual hall block, the western tower, and the chemise after about 1283. Together, the structures probably comprised the main residential range. The hall block, which projected beyond and stood on top of the north-western wall, formed a sideways E-plan, its two square towers projecting outward at either end of the rectangular hall chamber. Sadly, most of the hall has decayed, perhaps having been slighted during the Civil War; a portion of its inner wall still stands two storeys.

The western tower, which stands in front of the keep, survives in fairly good condition. Another square tower with rounded angles, the battlemented structure rose three storeys and probably provided comfortable accommodation. The Royal Commission state that, more than likely, the first floor served as the solar, or the lord's

private chamber. Besides access to a latrine turret, the tower also featured windows, stone stairs, and two elaborate round-backed fireplaces. A now vanished 'central tower' may have been larger than the western tower; it probably contained substantial living quarters for the de Penres household or their guests.

The two-storey chemise faces into the inner ward. Said to have been a defensive structure, the crescent-shaped building resembled a forebuilding and still rises about halfway up the eastern side of the keep. The chemise actually functioned like a fighting platform from which defenders could fire down upon attackers. Its location inside the castle prompts speculation about its real purpose; apparently, there was need for an added sense of security or stability around this vital part of the castle.

In 1322, Sir Robert de Penres joined the barons' rebellion against Hugh le Despenser, service for which was rewarded with his appointment as keeper of Haverfordwest Castle, in Pembrokeshire. De Penres was later arrested and investigated for his alleged role in the plunder of Edward II's treasure, a portion of which was apparently placed in his care, but he was released without charge. He became deputy justiciar of South Wales and, in 1336, acquired land in Llansteffan, Carmarthenshire.

Penrice Castle passed to Sir Richard de Penres, Robert's eldest brother, who in turn passed it to his son, another Robert. When this Robert de Penres married Elizabeth de Camville, the heiress to Llansteffan Castle, he brought that important property into the family. In 1377, Robert de Penres was convicted for the murder of a local woman, and the de Penres properties passed to Rhys ap Gruffydd. It took another 14 years for the rightful de Penres heir to regain control of both Penrice and Llansteffan Castles.

Sir John, the last male heir to the de Penres lineage, died childless in 1410. His sister, Isabella Mansel, inherited Penrice and Oxwich Castles, which in turn passed by right of marriage to her husband, Hugh. Philip Mansel, their grandson, acquired both castles when he reached adulthood in 1459. In 1463, Penrice Castle passed to Richard Penres, a relative of Philip Mansel's. In 1534, Sir Rice Mansel leased Penrice Castle to William Benet, whose family held it for the next 135 years. It was during this time that the dovecote was built and other minor additions were made to the castle.

The Mansels continued to own Penrice Castle and the surrounding estates until the 20th century. In the late 18th century, Thomas Mansel Talbot admired the location as 'the most romantic spot in all the county'. He built what he considered a stylish house just below the castle site, saving the ruins for ambience while also constructing the sham ruins at the main entrance on the A4118.

Today, the Methuen-Campbells, descendants of Thomas Mansel Talbot, own and occupy Penrice Castle. The overgrowth of ivy and other vegetation indicates the relatively fragile condition of the site, and prompt consolidation work is essential to prevent any further decay. According to representatives at Cadw, the funds are available to provide assistance if the owners wish to make structural improvements.

Pen-y-Pil

A much overgrown ringwork
Location: In the grounds of St. Illtyd's School in north-eastern
Cardiff (ST 227 804)
Access: On private ground

Labelled on the OS map as 'Cae Castell' and listed as 'Cae'r Castell' by the Royal Commission, the ringwork known as Pen-y-Pil can be seen from the Newport Road as a tree clad, fenced-off enclosure just to the west of the main buildings of St. Illtyd's School.

Unfortunately, historical records do not identify its original builder or history. Though located so close to Cardiff, the castle was actually part of the lordship of Gwynllwg and administered from Newport Castle.

The circular site stretched some 33 metres across. The ring-bank is highest on the north side and the main entrance stands to the east. There is no evidence of a bailey. A trench dug in 1965 revealed that a timber structure may have stood on the site; potsherds dating to the 12th century were also unearthed.

Peterston

Elements of stonework survive
Location: Alongside Peterston's village street, Peterston itself
lying about 7 miles west of the centre of Cardiff (ST 084 764)
Access: Can be easily seen from the road

Take the M4 to exit 334. Head south on the minor road and about half
a mile before you would reach the A48, turn left on the even more
minor road to Peterston-super-Ely. The cluster of remains stands on

the right hand side of the road after you enter the village and shortly before the post office is reached on the left hand side.

Much of what is known about Peterston Castle derives from the interpretation of a few fragments of masonry rather than from extensive excavation. Located not too far from the River Ely, which flows to the south, the site itself is fairly low-lying. From the three groups of ruins that survive, archaeologists have surmised that Peterston Castle was probably a rectangular enclosure castle with several wall towers and a large square keep, which may have been the first structure built at the site, probably in the 12th century.

The castle has almost completely disappeared, but some remnants have been incorporated into one of the four houses that stand on the medieval site. Of those, Caehir House contains a fine length of the wall that once formed the western side of a rectangular tower. More than likely, the eastern wall was used as building material for or torn down during construction of the house. The western wall still features a splayed window and putlog holes, and remnants of the latrine chute occupy the southern side, where part of a spiral staircase also survives. One can view the structure, which is more substantial than a first glance indicates, from the driveway of Caehir House. Remnants of the keep are more difficult to identify, but they do survive in the midst of the cluster of houses, just a bit south and west of Castelby House.

Peterston Castle apparently formed the centre of the demesne lordship of the le Sores, who acquired the manor in the early 12th century. The le Sores continued to hold Peterston Castle until the late 14th century, when they sold a portion of the site to Edward, Lord Despenser; the rest passed to John Butler by 1382. By the mid-15th century, the Butlers sold a portion of their holding to the Mathews of Radyr. In 1545, Henry VIII granted the Despenser share of the estate to John Thomas Basset, who in turn passed it to the Mansels and Aubreys. Some historians claim that the castle was targeted by Owain Glyndwr, who supposedly beheaded Sir Mayo (also called Sir Matho or Matthew) le Sore in 1402. However, nothing in the historical record supports this story; indeed the le Sores had already sold the property by then. By the time of Leland's visit in 1536, the castle had begun to decay.

Plas Baglan

Remains of very overgrown earthworks
Location: On the slopes above the eastern edge of Baglan, itself just north of Part Talbot (SS 756 923)
Access: On private ground with no public access

The ruins of what may have been a substantial masonry castle built by the Welsh Lords of Afan sometime in the 12th or 13th century survive in the midst of woodland east of Baglan. Even though nothing in the historical record documents the site's origins, it is quite possible that Morgan Gam owned the castle in the 13th century. The site reputedly developed into something of a cultural centre and during the 15th century became a favoured destination of bards and singers. Poet Dafydd ap Gwilym is said to have visited Plas Baglan on several occasions. Sixteenth-century records also refer to the castle, which was then probably called 'Courte Baglan'.

The Lewis or Thomas families lived at Plas Baglan until the very early 17th century, when they apparently abandoned the castle in favour of their new, more comfortable home at Baglan Hall (long since demolished). After the move, Plas Baglan fell into ruin. Ultimately, trees and other vegetation overtook the site, whilst much of the stonework was pilfered for building material for the nearby farmhouse at Ty Newydd Farm, now also ruined.

Today, Plas Baglan seems nothing more than a conglomeration of earthworks and bits of rubble. But the site once featured a substantial rectangular structure, probably a keep or a large first-floor hall, which stood on the north-western side of a rectangular platform formed by a ditch on the north and east and natural slopes on the remaining sides. At one time, the platform may have been defended by a mortared wall, traces of which are still visible. Surviving features include sections of thick walling and what may have been the castle's latrine turret. Several humps in the ground to the north-east of the site indicate the location of other buildings.

Plas Baglan is interesting not just as a Welsh-built castle but also as one of a cluster of medieval sites in the immediate area. Besides

Plas Baglan, another castle site – Castell Bolan – survives to the east, while in the village to the west, the parish church of St. Baglan features medieval relics, including early Christian carved stones, a double belfry, and well preserved windows dating to the 15th and 16th centuries.

Rumney
(Cae Castell)

The site is now occupied by new housing
Location: Just off the Newport road in north-eastern Cardiff
(ST 210 789)
Access: The 'site' above is visible from behind the
Oaklands Hotel

Turn off the Newport road in north-eastern Cardiff by the side of the Oaklands Hotel, and the site is under new housing at the rear of the hotel, perched above the Afon Rhymni. Like nearby Pen-y-Pil (otherwise known as Cae'r Castell), the castle at Rumney was originally located on the border between the lordships of Glamorgan and Gwynllwg, both of which Robert Fitzhamon controlled in the late 11th century. Rumney's Cae Castell may have been built by Robert de Haia, one of Robert Fitzhamon's close associates.

Having a fairly well documented history and having been the focus of extensive excavation in the late 1970s and early 1980s, much is known about the site. Rather than being either a Roman fort (as some OS maps indicate) or a motte, as the Royal Commission initially concluded, the structure was determined to consist of a ringwork which had manorial structures added to it in the 13th century. The ramparts still survive to a large degree despite the intrusion of a road (Castle Rise), houses, and tennis courts. To the south-west of the ringwork, an embanked area – probably the bailey – has been replaced with a car park.

Measuring 45 metres across the summit, Cae Castell was a formidable ringwork. A ditch enclosed the ringwork's more vulnerable southern, eastern, and northern sides. The castle was entered on the south-eastern side. Excavations revealed six building phases at the site. The first produced a partial ring-bank with a metalled inner courtyard, timber ramparts, a simple gate tower, a timber revetment on the south-eastern side, and another timber building on the northern side. A substantial timber gatehouse, a stone-and-timber revetment, and a six-bay timber hall (on the north) were

192

added during the second phase. These two phases lasted from about 1100 to the middle of the 12th century

Phase three involved the construction of more substantial defences, including a square keep, which was embedded into the eastern ramparts. Built with limestone, the keep had a paved floor and herringbone masonry. Two other buildings were also added at this time, one immediately to the left of the gateway and a second across the courtyard. They may have been built in response to the Welsh rebellion of 1184. Archaeological evidence suggests that the structure nearest the gateway may have served as a kitchen.

In the early 13th century during phase four, a new hall with at least six bays and two rooms replaced the original hall. A well or cistern was also added near the kitchen range, and a sturdy stone revetment buttressed the embankment between the gateway and the keep. Following closely upon phase four, phase five included the demolition of the original gateway and the construction of a new limestone replacement tower.

During the 1290s, Rumney Castle was converted into a fine residence. The earthen ramparts on the east were lowered at this time and a long hall block built in their place. A new building, possibly used for smelting, was built on the site of the hall and the main entrance was narrowed. A rectangular structure was built into the eastern wall; its function is uncertain. The circular building located to the west of the gate tower may have served as a signal beacon or a lime kiln. Archaeologists have since discovered a hoard of Edwardian era coins dating to 1295.

Early in the 12th century, control of the castle passed to Earl Robert FitzRoy of Gloucester, Lord of Glamorgan, along with the entire lordship of Gwynllwg. From then until its destruction, Rumney Castle remained the property of the Lords of Glamorgan, who used constables to administer the castle for them. The conversion of the site into a manorial centre (phases four and five) probably took place during the lordship of Gilbert de Clare III, when his mother, Joan, had control of the castle. Evidence suggests that Cae Castell was targeted by Morgan ap Maredudd, whose followers destroyed it shortly after 1295. Although the manor recovered, the castle was never restored.

Ruperra (Rhiwperra)

A motte with fine all-encompassing views, with a modern wall
Location: 5 miles east of Caerphilly (ST 223 867)
Access: Can be reached by a good stroll on public footpaths

Take the A469 from the north-east of Caerphilly towards Newport. Beyond Machen (in Lower Machen), take the minor road right to Draethen. Park near the Hollybush Inn, and take the footpath that leads across a stile just to the right of the inn, and which then turns left and uphill across a field to a gate into the woodland. Carry on up the path, crossing a crossroads of paths, and then turn right when you meet a T-junction with a bridleway. Walk along this for a few hundred yards, and then fork left onto the next footpath. At a further crossroads of paths near the crest of the ridge, turn left and carry on uphill along the ridge. In due course you will reach the motte. Much of the site is engulfed by trees, but, fortunately, the motte has been cleared for ongoing restoration work and is quite accessible.

Erected on top of Coed Craig, a ridge not too far east of Caerphilly, Ruperra was well appointed to watch the activity on the Afon Rhymni, which flows along the northern and eastern sides around the base of the ridge. Rising about 6 metres, the motte was located in the north-east corner of an Iron Age hillfort, the ramparts of which would have offered extra protection. Around its perimeter, the motte was also defended by a ditch and counterscarping. In the 18th century, the Morgan family apparently built a summerhouse on the summit of the motte, but, today, only a bit of its stone pathway survives.

No historical records have been identified for the castle, also known as Castell Breiniol (according to Iolo Morgannwg), Castell-y-Ddraenen, and Coed Craig-Ruperra. There is evidence that the Welsh occupied the area until the mid-13th century, and the castle itself was probably abandoned by the 14th century. Although historians believe the motte was of Norman rather than Welsh origins, control of the castle may have alternated between the Welsh and Norman overlords.

At the time of writing, the Ruperra Trust had undertaken extensive restoration work on the original Norman castle, buttressing its eroding base and terraced hillsides and also consolidating the masonry. Archaeologists working with the Trust have discovered medieval-looking walls under the surface of the motte, as well as some medieval pottery, and have recommended a proper excavation of the site.

St. Donats

A castle continuously inhabited since the 12th century, now a college

Location: In the village of St. Donats, 2 miles west of Llantwit Major (SS 935 681)

Access: Access to the site is allowed only during summer months and when the college has closed for holidays. Visitors are then welcome to freely wander the grounds and to enter the inner ward of the castle, but the interiors are off limits. However, parts can be viewed from the track leading down to the church below the castle

Atlantic College is difficult to miss in this small village, and is one of Glamorgan's finest medieval castles. There is parking close to the castle, from where the track also leads down to the church. This contains a 12th-century chancel arch and font. A 14th-century chapel contains marble monuments to several Stradling family members, including Sir Edward Stradling V and Sir Thomas Stradling III.

As a result of almost continuous occupation since the 12th century, its present use as a college, and the impressive restoration work done in the late 19th and 20th centuries, St. Donats Castle offers an outstanding opportunity to experience a castle as it may have looked in its heyday.

The layout of the present castle, coupled with the existence of the faceted curtain wall, indicates that a fairly large ringwork once occupied the site, probably in the late 12th century. Ultimately, St. Donats developed into a concentric castle, but, unlike Caerphilly, the design of which included concentric defences from the start, St. Donats evolved its concentric defences over time, as additions were made and the ringwork was refortified in stone.

The de Hawey family, who also owned estates in Somerset, chose an ideal spot to build their castle, situating it on the edge of a steep hillside with splendid views to the Bristol Channel. Later construction has long since obscured the earth and timber castle, which encompassed what is now the inner ward and walls of the castle. At St. Donats, the ringwork was extended to create a more formidable castle, one defended by an outer concentric ring and ditch. Interestingly, it was only relatively recently that archaeologists identified the medieval fabric of the castle. The surviving outer wall and ditch were built in the early 14th century, when the original ditch was probably in-filled to support the narrow area between the two gatehouses.

The first reliable record dates to 1262, when St. Donats was held by Thomas de Hawey II. Thomas II's heir, also named Thomas, died without a son in 1298, so his married sister, Joan Stradling, inherited St. Donats. Consequently, by right of marriage, Joan's Swiss-born husband, Sir Peter de Stratelynge (Stradling), became lord of the castle and the estates that accompanied it. Sir Peter died in about 1300, and ownership of the castle reverted to Joan, whose second husband, Sir John de Pembridge, held St. Donats during the minorities of the two Stradling sons, John and Edward.

By 1317, Edward Stradling had acquired the castle and began transforming the structure into a concentric fortress. Besides adding the outer walling and ditch and filling in the original ditch, Stradling probably built the fine outer gatehouse. He also strengthened the interior walls, replaced timber ramparts with stone, added three other towers along the interior walls, and upgraded the keep.

The Stradlings held onto St. Donats for several centuries. Three of the Stradlings (Sirs William, Edward III, and Henry) separately

The internal wall of the gatehouse

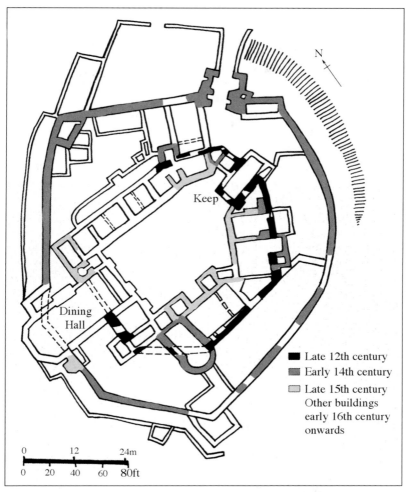

Keep

Dining
Hall

■ Late 12th century
■ Early 14th century
□ Late 15th century
　Other buildings
　early 16th century
　onwards

N

| 0 | | 12 | | 24m |
| 0 | 20 | 40 | 60 | 80ft |

journeyed to the Holy Land to participate in the Crusades; all
became Knights of the Holy Sepulchre. Sir Henry Stradling was
married to Elizabeth Herbert, the sister of the Earl of Pembroke.
The couple reputedly survived kidnapping by Breton pirates, led
by Colyn Dolphyn, who held them for ransom. Although legends
claim that the ruined watchtower on the opposite headland was
raised in response to the kidnapping and to lure the pirates to their
death on the rocks below, the structure was actually erected some

200 years after the event. One variation of the story claims that the locals actually buried Colyn Dolphyn in the sand beneath the tower, with hopes that the rising tide would drown him. On his way home from the Crusades in 1476, Sir Henry died in Cyprus.

Coming of age in about 1493, Edward Stradling IV became lord of St. Donats. Shortly after receiving a knighthood in 1513, Sir Edward initiated two major building programmes at the castle, adding the Gibbet Tower on the north-western corner, the huge great hall (known as Stradling Hall), and the north-eastern block of apartments. He also extended the south-eastern range of buildings to reach the keep. During the second building phase, Stradling completed the west and north domestic ranges and erected the Lady Anne Tower on the south-western corner of the outer ward. Most of what survives today directly dates to this time.

Edward's son, Sir Thomas Stradling II (1535-1571), led a chaotic existence at England's royal court. A devout Catholic, he was imprisoned in the Tower of London for making poor political choices in 1551 and was again sent to the Tower during the reign of Elizabeth I. After his release, Sir Thomas returned to St. Donats, where he lived out the rest of his life but continued to defy the Protestant queen's religious mandates.

Sir Edward Stradling V (1571-1609), whose impressive library at St. Donats was widely renowned, was educated at Oxford and involved in politics. He became a Member of Parliament at the age 25, served as Sheriff of Glamorgan, and was an influential justice of the peace. At St. Donats, Sir Edward V added a long gallery, expanded the western range with three projecting bays and elaborately decorated plasterwork ceilings, erected a brewhouse alongside the outer gate, and built several buildings in the outer ward. His legacy includes the creation of a historical pedigree for the family, one that documented blood ties back to Sir William le Esterling, one of the 12 Norman knights who supposedly conquered Glamorgan. In the 20th century, historians debunked Stradling's fancied ancestry.

Dying childless, Sir Edward V's property passed to Sir John Stradling II, a direct descendant of Sir Thomas Stradling I. Sir John was a powerful political force who served as Glamorgan's sheriff and deputy-lieutenant and as a Member of Parliament from 1623 to

1626. His son, yet another Edward, sided with the Royalists during the English Civil War and led a regiment at the Battle of Edgehill. He died at Oxford in 1644. St. Donats passed to Sir Edward Stradling VIII and his son, Sir Edward IX. Another Edward, the eldest son, was slated to acquire the family's castle but died before his father, and the castle passed to Sir Edward's second son, Thomas.

The Stradlings continued to live at St. Donats Castle until 1738, when Sir Thomas Stradling III died in France during a duel and was returned to St. Donats for burial. Aged only 25 and childless, Thomas had agreed with a friend, Sir John Tyrwhitt, that, if either died before the other, the survivor would inherit the other's property. For some time, the pledge remained unfulfilled, but, in 1755, Tyrwhitt finally acquired St. Donats. Ironically, he never lived at the grand castle. One Stradling story says that Sir Thomas' body was in fact never returned to St Donats and that, in reality, an impostor's corpse, still bearing all ten fingers (one of Stradling's had been eaten by a donkey), was buried in his place. Some people believed the nine-fingered Thomas would one day return to reclaim his inheritance, but, of course, he never did. Unfortunately, Sir Edward V's marvellous library was dispersed at this time and the collection has been lost. In time, the castle passed to Tyrwhitt family members and then was abandoned.

In 1862, claiming he was descended from the Stradlings, Dr. John Whitlock Nicholl-Carne bought the estate and began the castle's rebirth. In 1901, after Nicholl-Carne's death, Morgan Stuart Williams purchased the structure and continued restoring the castle. In 1922, Richard Pennoyer bought the castle, but sold it three years later to William Randolph Hearst, the American newspaper magnate. Hearst hired architect Charles Allom to complete the transformation of the castle into one of the world's great showcases.

St. Donats simple rectangular outer gatehouse spanned a dry ditch and was defended by several arrowslits, a portcullis, murder holes, and battlements. The presence of a recessed archway in front of the gate passage indicates that a wooden turning bridge was once used to defend the castle. Now, a stone pathway flanked by short battlemented walls allows access to the interior. Situated in the centre of the archway, a carved medallion (dating to the 1960s) has replaced the original Stradling arms that adorned the spot. The two lancet-headed windows probably lit the first-floor windlass room, which may also have served as the constable's chamber. A cross-oillet is visible at the roofline.

The faceted curtain wall combined long straight stretches of battlemented wall with angle towers to give the illusion that the wall was curved. The effect is easy to make out to the left of the gatehouse. Putlog holes indicate where medieval scaffolding was held in place during construction.

The pathway around the left side of the castle not only takes visitors to the fine views afforded by the location, but also allows a closer look at the lush gardens – and two of the castle's most recent yet notable structures. The Bradenstoke Hall encompasses almost the entire southern side of the castle. Extensively restored by William Randolph Hearst, who transported the impressive roof and quatrefoil windows from their original setting at Bradenstoke Priory in Wiltshire, the grand scale of this modern structure reflects the status of the great newspaper baron.

Immediately beyond the Bradenstoke Hall stands the Lady Anne Tower. Entirely rebuilt by Hearst, the tall rectangular tower actually replaced one from the 14th century; it incorporates masonry from the earlier tower and other pieces imported from abroad. Together, the Lady Anne Tower and the Bradenstoke Hall look more like a church than a modern residential range. Another corner tower stands at the north-western angle of the outer curtain wall. Contemporary with the outer gatehouse, brewhouse, and outer curtain wall, most of this northern tower is now obscured by modern buildings.

Between the curtain wall and the interior of the castle, a narrow, partially cobbled area covers the site of the original ditch. The restored brewhouse stands to the right of the outer gateway, the inner façade of which is adorned by a carved figure – said to be that of King Edward III – embedded in a roundel. On the opposite side of the cobbled yard, the plain gateway provides access to the inner courtyard; it probably replaced the original timber entrance to the Norman ringwork.

Recognising the weaknesses inherent in the simple gateway, the Stradlings constructed a rectangular keep on its southern side;

the combination of structures is reminiscent of other ringworks in Glamorganshire, such as Newcastle Bridgend, which also had a faceted curtain wall. Sometimes known as the Mansel Tower, the tall, battlemented keep projects both into the inner courtyard and outward into the outer ward. It contained a ground-level storage chamber, a first-floor hall and upper-level residential chamber, a spiral staircase, a latrine turret, and mullioned and Norman-era windows. Access to the interior is presently restricted.

Regularly refortified from the late 12th through the 16th centuries and modified during the 20th century by Hearst, the inner curtain wall, which was faceted and battlemented, replaced the ringwork's original timber ramparts. Facing the courtyard, the austere wall on the rear of the keep is graced with a roundel depicting the controversial Roman emperor, Caligula. One of four at the castle, the medallion was originally part of a set of 12 terracotta roundels made for Hampton Court Palace in 1521. Sir Edward Stradling IV apparently acquired the objects from Sir Thomas Arundell, his father-in-law, who was an associate of Cardinal Wolsey. Wolsey had commissioned the artwork for his palace prior to its acquisition by Henry VIII.

By the end of the 16th century, the inner ward functioned more as a grand Tudor manor house, but it was still fairly well protected by its medieval defences. The Gibbet Tower still stands four storeys tall on the north-western side of the inner wall between the west and north ranges of buildings; a stair turret allowed movement between the tower and the western range. A rectangular tower guarded the inner ward at the south-eastern corner, and a round tower defended the south-west. Portions survive, albeit largely incorporated into the later castle.

Several impressive buildings enclose the inner ward. Each has been extensively renovated, yet still reflects both medieval and Renaissance origins. Atlantic College administrators occupy several of the structures and others provide student accommodation.

Lining the south-eastern side of the castle courtyard adjacent to the keep, the south-eastern block, which contained the service rooms, now largely dates to the late 15th and early 16th centuries. Immediately to the left is the large Stradling Hall, erected at the same time. Of particular note is the fine porchway, which was the main entrance into the battlemented great hall. It is adorned with an impressive oriel window and also features two lion-headed spouts. Another oriel window is located on the opposite end of the hall. Stradling Hall contains a noteworthy long gallery, which once spanned the first floor but has long since been divided into several rooms.

The two-storey northern range provided accommodation for the Stradlings, Hearst, and various dignitaries, including David Lloyd George. Even though extensively renovated by Hearst, the buildings retain several original features, including the battlements and the five-arched windows dressed with Sutton stone that overlook the inner ward. A roundel bearing the Stradling arms is situated above the main doorway.

Rebuilt by Hearst to house the elaborate dining hall and breakfast room on the ground floor and a magnificent armoury above, the three-bayed western range connects the northern and southern ranges. The earliest range of buildings on this spot was used for domestic purposes; it held private apartments and a smaller hall reserved for the lord. The college library now occupies the first floor. Two roundels, also part of the Hampton Court Palace set, adorn the walls facing into the courtyard; one features Emperor Marcus Aurelius and the other is said to be Cleopatra.

When Hearst bankrupted himself in the 1930s, St. Donats Castle was again put up for sale, but the Second World War intervened and the site became a military training centre. Finally, in 1960, the property was purchased for use as a college, and, in 1962, Atlantic College opened to students from around the world.

St. Fagans

An Elizabethan mansion incorporates curtain walling and elements of layout from an earlier castle
Location: In the centre of St. Fagans, 4 miles west of the centre of Cardiff (ST 120 772)
Access: Free admission to the house and grounds, which is part of the National Museum

St. Fagans is well signposted and easily reached from the A4232 that swings round the west of Cardiff.

Historians believe a ringwork castle may have occupied this site as early as the late 11th century, when the le Sore family acquired the estate in exchange for one knight's service. More than likely, Robert le Sore erected an earth and timber castle in the very late 11th century or early 12th century. The D-shaped curtain wall, which forms the southern side of the site, may trace the layout of the original castle. The le Sores held St. Fagans Castle until 1300, when it passed by right of marriage to the le Vele family. The le

Veles in turn occupied the castle until 1411, when the Welsh seized the site during the Glyndwr rebellion.

By 1429, Richard Beauchamp, Lord of Glamorgan, had regained control of St. Fagans and served as its custodian during the minority of the le Vele heir. The le Vele family held the castle until the male line died out and the heiress, Alice le Vele, married David Mathew. In the 1560s, Mathew's heiresses sold the decaying castle to Dr. John Gibbon. Shortly thereafter, Gibbon may have erected the Elizabethan house that still stands on the castle site. There is speculation, however, that Nicholas Herbert, who purchased the castle from Gibbon, may have actually built the house in the 1580s or 1590s. In any case, the Herberts sold St. Fagans to Sir Edward Lewis of the Van (Y Fan) near Caerphilly in 1616. Moving from the Van, Sir Edward's descendants used St. Fagans as their main residence until 1730, when it was acquired by the Earls of Plymouth by right of marriage.

The le Sore castle was ideally poised to watch over the activity on the River Ely which flows to the south. On its western and southern sides, steep escarpments still flank the property. It is here where visitors can identify the surviving portion of the faceted medieval curtain wall, which averages about 1.8 metres in thickness. The wall-walk still rises over 3 metres. A small sally port also survives at the south-western corner of the wall. The northern length of curtain wall was removed and its ditch infilled in the 16th century when the castle's Elizabethan transformation took place. Today's entrance faces east, as it probably did during the Middle Ages.

Since the Elizabethan residence is not a true castle, only brief mention will be made of notable architectural features. Rising two storeys, the overall design is E-shaped, which was typical of the times. The ground level of the southern wing holds a huge kitchen and two dressed-stone fireplaces. Located near the centre of the house, the hall features elaborate panelling and friezework, heraldic emblems, and a marvellous chimneypiece. The stunning drawing room in the northern wing displays fine plasterwork, additional ornate friezework, and tapestries. At first-floor level, skilfully carved ornamentation and tapestries adorn the walls of the long gallery and other, smaller rooms.

In the early 19th century St. Fagans Castle was used as a farmhouse and its condition deteriorated. Fortunately, during the 1850s, the structure was restored. In 1946, the Earls of Plymouth donated the castle to the National Museum of Wales, which in turn transformed the property into an impressive open-air museum.

St. Georges

Any remains have been incorporated into Church Farm
Location: In the middle of St. George's, to the west of Cardiff
Access: Castle Farm can be seen from the road

Castle Farm sits in the midst of the village, above the railway level crossing and about ½ mile west of the small cruciform parish church, which dates to the 14th century. Quite possibly, the church and castle were erected at about the same time.

While little physical evidence survives to prove the existence of a castle in the midst of what is now the village of St. Georges-super-Ely, the name 'Castle Farm', traces of earthworks, and historical documents all point to the likelihood that a fortified residence of some sort originally occupied this spot. What does survive is a fine example of a medieval first-floor hall, most of which dates to the 15th century. The thickness of the hall's north and west walls varies from 1.7 to 2.3 metres; quite possibly, these walls may have formed part of an older, defended structure which the hall replaced.

The origins of the present structure, which is perched at the edge of a slope and overlooks the River Ely, are somewhat hazy. More than likely, it was erected by the Fleming family, who acquired the manor of St. George's in about 1317. By the end of the century, St. George's passed to Sir Thomas Malefant, heir to the Fleming inheritance through his grandmother, Margaret Malefant (see also Llanmaes Castle). In the 16th century, Jasper Tudor acquired the property. After his death, the Herberts, Earls of Pembroke, held the site. In the 18th century, the Lords Windsor sold St. Georges to Abraham Barbour.

Ultimately, the Trahernes acquired the site. Rumours that Owain Glyndwr may have destroyed the castle are unsubstantiated; but, it is possible, considering that Castle Farm dates to that time period and may have been built to replace the earlier castle. Interestingly, the earthworks to the south-west of the farmhouse contain fragments of stone buildings; the ditch beyond may have defended the site.

St. Nicholas Gaer

> A fine example of a ringwork
> Location: Just north of St. Nicholas, itself about 7 miles east of
> Cowbridge along the A48 (ST 084 875)
> Access: A track passes close by to the west

To reach this fine ringwork, park near the Presbyterian church in St. Nicholas (signposted off the A48). Walk on up the track that runs alongside the church and away from the A48. This soon bends left, then right. When a path leads off over a stile straight ahead, keep to the track as it bends right and then left again. As it crests the ridge the ringwork can be seen to the right, marked by the presence of a Scots pine. (If you return to the stile just mentioned, and cross over the it, you can see the site of Cotterell Castle (see p.82). This lies at right angles to your left as you cross the stile, in a clump of trees about 300 metres away on a slight promontory.)

Also known as Y Gaer, St. Nicholas Gaer is an excellent example of a ringwork. Except for some low-lying bracken and a few trees, the site is fairly accessible. Visitors can walk around almost the entire ring-bank, which extends approximately 52 metres by 44 metres. Around the exterior, a well preserved ditch once defended the castle. A short counterscarp embankment can be identified on the eastern side.

The largest of three timber castles erected near St. Nicholas village, this ringwork probably served as caput for the Corbet family, whose involvement in the Norman subjugation of Glamorgan dates at least to the 12th century. By 1262, William Corbet had control of the three knight's fees at St. Nicholas. The historical record documents two raids on the castle, the first when Welsh burned the castle in 1226, and another three years later, when Hywel ap Maredudd of Meisgyn destroyed the site. Its owners promptly repaired the castle and used it into the following century. Then, the Flemings of nearby St. Georges purchased the castle; the Malefants acquired the site in the 1320s.

Stormy

A large but low motte
Location: 3 miles west of Bridgend (SS 846 815)
Access: A footpath leads round the south of the site, but because of the open fields, the motte is clearly visible on the skyline

It is easiest to locate this motte by starting in Pyle. Take the B4281 east towards Kenfig Hill and at the traffic light controlled cross-roads towards the edge of the town, turn right. Follow this road and once across the railway line you want to park near where the road bends slightly to the left. On the right-hand side of the road on the bend you will find a stone stile which leads to a footpath that runs on slightly higher ground left of a hedgerow boundary which it shadows across the hillside at roughly right angles to the road. Well before you reach the next field boundary you will see the motte on the skyline to your right.

The low-lying motte once watched activity on the Port Way, which the motorway now traces through the area. The motte itself is fairly flat; its summit spans over 15 metres. There are no signs of a bailey.

In the 12th century, the compact site served as the caput of the Sturmi family, who founded Sturmieston, or *Villa Sturmi*. By the early 13th century, the Sturmis had donated their lands to Margam Abbey and abandoned their castle shortly afterwards. The turf-covered ruins of what are probably the remains of these buildings are clearly visible south-east of the motte.

Sully

Vanished from view (ST 152 683)

Less than a mile east of Barry, the village of Sully is best accessed via the B4267. The castle site is located immediately east of the parish church behind the public house. There are no visible remains.

Regrettably, Sully Castle has completely vanished from view, the development of a housing estate having done considerable damage to the site in the early 1970s. Fortunately, officials had enough foresight to require excavation of the site before construction began, and much about the medieval stronghold was documented. Underneath the later masonry structures, archaeologists identified a short, weak section of a bank and ditch. Enough of this embankment remained for them to determine that the first castle on the site was not a masonry courtyard castle, as initially believed, but rather a notable ringwork.

Evidently, Sully's ringwork was typical of its time and may have looked much like Newcastle or Coity did in their early stages. As at the other ringworks, Sully's rectangular stone keep appears to have been situated just to the left of the castle's main entrance. Its foundations were unearthed during the 1960s and also during earlier excavations carried out in the mid-19th century, when G.T. Clark recorded the site. It was evidently extended for use as the lord's private residence during the 13th century. Remains of four other structures dating to the mid- to late-12th century were also discovered inside what would have been the original ringwork. A drystone revetment was added at about the same time.

The ringwork was possibly built by Reginald de Sully or one of his immediate descendants, who held the caput of Sully from the late 11th century until the death of Raymond de Sully, the last of the male line, in about 1317. In the 13th century, Walter de Sully gained considerable power within the lordship of Glamorgan; for a time during the minority of Gilbert de Clare II, he served as custodian of the lordship.

Raymond de Sully may have been responsible for the construction of the second 'castle' at Sully, a structure apparently more akin

212

to a stronghouse or fortified manor than a castle in the truest sense of the word. Built around the ringwork, the new 'castle' featured a five-sided enclosing wall which measured less than 2 metres in thickness; a meagre gateway opened near the north-west corner. In the late 13th or early 14th century, a large hall was added on the eastern side of the ringwork and another complex of buildings appeared on the south-west. Superseding the keep, they probably served as the castle's main administrative and domestic centres.

By the 1340s, the de Sullys had left the castle, and ownership passed to the Despensers. The castle later reverted to the monarchy, and, in time, passed to Sir Thomas Stradling. The Stradlings, whose main seat was at St. Donats, continued to own Sully Castle until 1738, when it passed to the Mansels. They in turn managed the estate until 1780. An Act of Parliament was required to settle the dispute over who would next control the castle, and both St. Donats and Sully were granted to Sir John de la Fountaine Tyrwhitt. His descendants, the Drakes, held Sully Castle until 1811, when Evan Thomas purchased the site.

In 1838, Sully Castle was bought by the Guest family, who probably sponsored the archaeological work done there by G.T. Clark. In 1914, the estate and its possessions were sold at private auction, and the site was neglected until its excavation in the 1960s.

The neighbouring parish church of St. John the Baptist stands on the site of an earlier Norman foundation, traces of which were uncovered during 19th-century restoration work. The battlemented tower dates to the 15th century.

Swansea

Substantial stonework remains
Location: At the eastern end of the main shopping centre
(SS 657 931)
Access: The external walls can be viewed readily

Sadly, modern construction has encroached upon the medieval castle at Swansea, dwarfing the ruins and destroying much of the site. Access is presently restricted because of the castle's precarious position in the midst of the bustling city centre and its ruinous condition.

Shortly after Henry de Beaumont, Earl of Warwick, acquired the lordship of Gower (Gwyr) from Henry I in the early 12th century, he ordered the construction of the motte and bailey castle that became the caput, or administrative centre, of his lordship. At the same time, he also began work on the adjacent borough, which eventually spread around the castle. As late as the 18th century, substantial remains of the motte still occupied the site – the prolific Buck Brothers not only depicted a tree-topped mound just north of the ruins but also clearly displayed why the original Norman builders chose the site to begin with: the River Tawe flowed eastward close to the base of the castle. All action on the river could be monitored from the castle which dominated the clifftop above. The river also functioned as a harbour.

In the late 19th century, Lt. Col. William Llewelyn Morgan examined the site and determined that the Norman castle probably occupied the land between Castle Walls Lane and Castle Bailey Street, which run north/south. He believed the embankments forming the bailey enclosed a roughly rectangular area running along Welcome Lane and College Street on the north, Goat Street on the west, Caer Street and Castle Lane on the south, and Castle Walls Lane on the east. Since then, the street plan of Swansea has been altered so much that most of the Norman site has been obliterated. The motte itself was destroyed in 1913, when a large block of buildings was constructed on top of the site.

Lt. Col. Morgan also identified remnants of the bailey's bank and ditch, the existence of which was confirmed by Bernard Morris in 1975. Morris noted that the west ditch was flat-bottomed, measured about 3.6 metres deep and 10.4 metres wide, and contained several 13th- and 14th-century potsherds from the later stone castle.

The first mention of Swansea Castle in the historical record dates to 1116, when the Welsh, led by Gruffydd ap Rhys, assaulted the stronghold, burning the bailey ramparts but not capturing the castle. Some speculation exists that the Welsh actually held the castle for a brief time shortly after Gruffydd's attack, but by 1138, when Henry de Neubourgh seized the Gower and regained the lordship, the Normans were firmly back in control. Henry de Neubourgh adopted the name 'de Gower' (*Henricus de Goher*) and refortified Swansea Castle, which again became the lordship's caput. One of the castle's important roles was as a mint. De Gower's nephew, Earl William of Warwick, inherited the lordship and issued Swansea's first borough charter.

Mike Salter notes that evidence of a fire at the castle was unearthed during construction work in 1913. He suggests that this occurred either in the attack in 1116 mentioned above or perhaps in an assault in 1192, when Rhys ap Gruffydd besieged Swansea, then commanded by William de Londres. Although Rhys continued the assault for some ten weeks, the Welsh never captured the castle.

Throughout the early 13th century, the Welsh, led by Rhys Gryg, his brother Maelgwyn and Rhys Ieuanc, continued their assaults on the castle and also stormed much of the Gower Peninsula. In 1215, they successfully attacked and burned Swansea, and probably seized the castle. The borough, which was also assaulted, was actually destroyed by the garrison, who set it alight to thwart the Welsh. In 1217, the Welsh again attacked Swansea, destroyed the castle, and wrested the lordship from Reginald de Braose. Shortly afterwards, John de Braose regained control and began refortifying the castle with stone.

With Llywelyn ab Iorwerth's rise to power, conflict escalated between the Welsh and their Anglo-Norman overlords. The

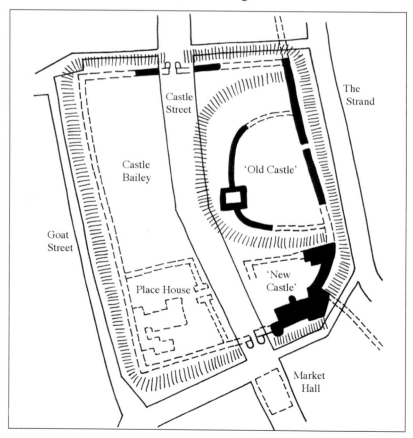

ongoing threat of rebellion led to the construction of more substantial defences at Swansea, and, by the end of the century, the so-called 'New Castle' finally appeared to the south of the motte site. The name, 'New Castle', is something of a misnomer, for rather than building a completely different stronghold to supplant the more rudimentary motte castle, the de Braose family actually enclosed the original site with a stone curtain wall. At the south-eastern corner, they added the elaborate hall block — complete with a kitchen range to the west and a solar to the east — which is now largely ruined. The entire range of structures was extensively altered over time.

Visible castle ruins include the battlemented remains of the two-storey de Braose hall block and service buildings facing south along Castle Lane; a taller, round latrine tower and spiral stairway at the westernmost end; and a square residential building with the solar, which projected slightly outward past the hall block on the eastern end. Extending northward from the eastern corner, a length of curtain wall connected the solar block to the square north-eastern tower. This tower was possibly first used to house the garrison, but in more recent times it served as a debtor's prison.

Viewable only from the exterior, the de Braose hall block features three barrel-vaulted basements, each lit by a cross-oillet. The great hall, recognisable by its two large pointed windows, spans most of the first floor. To the left, a smaller, double-light window trimmed with Sutton stone identifies the location of the service room. Interestingly, access to the first floor could only be accomplished by using a staircase that led from the inner courtyard; it was not until the late Middle Ages that a spiral staircase was added to ease movement between the levels. A residential chamber occupied the level over the service room; it is now mainly notable for its fireplace, windows with seats, and a narrow passage linking it to a round latrine tower, which supported a small observation post. Two gunloops, possibly added during restoration work carried out in the 1640s, survive on the uppermost level of the latrine tower.

The ornate eastern range extends north-east from the hall. The rectilinear block of buildings contained what has tentatively been identified as the lesser hall or solar above another series of vaulted basements. The exact nature of the first-floor chamber remains unclear, but it probably served the private needs of the lord and his family. A sub-basement supported the chambers on the floors above and also offered access to the River Tawe. The ground level basements were lit with trefoil-headed lancet windows dressed with Sutton stone. Of the two basements, the northern one may have held the brewhouse or a workroom, whereas the angular southern room would have provided extra storage. A 19th-century candle-making factory evidently replaced much of the medieval masonry at this corner of the castle, where a large fireplace and ovens were also located. Surviving features include a mural staircase, a neatly hidden garderobe, trefoil windows, and Sutton stone dressings.

The highlight of both blocks of buildings is the impressive arcade which decorates the parapet alongside the wall-walk where it stretches across the hall block and eastern range. Eleven open arches span the hall block; another five closed, or blind, arches adorn the east range on its south side; and eight more rim the eastern façade. Besides their decorative function, the arches encouraged rainwater run-off from the rooftop.

The similarity of these arches to the arcades adorning the two Pembrokeshire bishops' palaces at St. Davids and Lamphey is striking. However, although historians once believed that Bishop Gower occupied Swansea Castle and, therefore, was responsible for constructing these arches as well as those he built in Pembrokeshire, there is no documentation to support this notion. Rather, it is reasonable to assume that the bishop may have offered the de Mowbrays, Lords of Gower, the services of his masons, who were working nearby on the construction of the Hospital of the Blessed David in 1332. Perhaps they were influenced by Bishop Gower's architectural penchant for arcading.

The unassuming north-eastern tower completes the trio of castle buildings surviving from the Middle Ages. Although greatly altered over time as its function changed, the tower retains several medieval features, including cross-oillets, three ground-level vaulted basements, window-arches, and decorative mouldings. The narrowest of the three chambers probably served as the castle's cesspit. During the late 18th century, when the tower contained the debtor's prison, four cells were added over the basement. Each was equipped with a small round-backed fireplace and heavy doors, which survive. The debtor's prison closed in 1858.

In some ways, Swansea Castle was more like a walled town that held some heavily defended buildings, including the lord's residence and the lordship's administrative facility, than it was a castle. Essentially, the castle consisted of a large enclosed area, a typical bailey reinforced in the 13th century with stone. It originally contained the motte, which was later supplanted by the south-eastern block of buildings discussed above. In the 14th century, Swansea became a moderately affluent borough and plots of land within the walled bailey and some of the wall towers were leased to burgesses and other tenants. By this time, however, the Lords of Gower had little interest in the castle and increasingly used it as a prison.

In 1322, Edward II appointed Hugh le Despenser as Lord of Gower, taking the lordship from the de Braoses in response to the participation of John de Mowbray (Alina de Braose's husband) in the failed barons' rebellion. Despenser imprisoned several local citizens for supporting de Mowbray, who had seized Swansea Castle and the lordship of Gower two years earlier. Despenser kept the prisoners in chains in the castle for four weeks, and then ransomed them — but only after he had seized their property. De Mowbray was executed for his role in the rebellion and the Battle of Boroughbridge, and his wife and son were sent to the Tower of London.

By 1399, when Richard II visited Swansea, the castle had already begun to decline. By 1410, Swansea Castle was declared to have no monetary value, even though its bridges, towers, gates, houses, and walls were rebuilt. Curiously, even though the Welsh under Glyndwr controlled most of the Gower, they apparently never bothered to assault Swansea.

During the mid-15th century, new buildings were added to the castle site, including New Place, an impressive mansion built for Mathew Cradock, who then served as the castle's constable. Though the south-eastern range was retained for use by the Lord of Gower, during the 16th century it also served as a prison and was the site of several executions.

While the associated town continued to prosper and expand, Swansea Castle fell into ruin after Henry Somerset's death in 1549. Repairs were made sporadically, but, in 1647, Parliamentarian troops were ordered to slight the castle. Despite its ruinous condition, the site later was leased to Captain Thomas Jones, and then to Matthew Davyes. Within 30 years, Robert Wilmott and John Man established a glassworks inside the castle and produced wine bottles at their factory.

Other alterations to the castle included the construction of a copper works in the 18th century; the conversion of the hall block into a poor house; demolition of parts of the curtain wall to make way for a new market; use of the hall block to house the militia and function as a drill room; and, in the 20th century, occupation by the *South Wales Evening Post*. Portions of the castle also served as a town hall, storage cellars, a smithy, a Roman Catholic chapel, and a dovecote.

The Somersets placed Swansea Castle in State care in 1957. Currently, Cadw owns and is responsible for maintaining the castle's visible remains. The City and County of Swansea owns the buried remains of the castle and the grassed areas around it.

Talybont

A motte
Location: 1 miles south-west of Pontardulais (SN 587 027)
Access: Can be approached by and seen from a public footpath

Take the B4296 south from Pontardulais towards Gorseinion. Cross over the motorway and then the railway and after another 200 metres or so take the take the unsignposted tarmacced lane off to the right. You can park ahead, where the lane bends to the right. Walk up the lane to the right (signposted to Castell-du) and turn right onto the footpath just before you reach the house, to walk up the stoned track. Once under the railway bridge you will see the gorse-clad motte ahead and slightly to the right, in a field and adjacent to the M4. If you know what you are looking for – and not driving – you should be able to see this motte from the west bound carriageway of the M4.

Variously called Llandeilo Talybont, Castell Du, Castell Hu, or Hugh's Castle, Castell Talybont was strategically placed to guard the southern side of the River Loughor. A second motte castle, Ystum Enlli, kept track of activity on the northern bank of the river, which is in Carmarthenshire.

While the exact origins of the motte and bailey are uncertain, most historians believe Henry de Villers probably built Castell Talybont in about 1107. It was well sited to defend the north-western fringes

221

of the new lordship of Gower, then headed by Henry de Beaumont, Earl of Warwick. The only motte castle in the lordship, Talybont was erected on top of a glacial deposit, similar to the mottes in Glamorgan.

In many ways, Talybont is a classic motte and bailey castle. The mound rises about 6 metres above ground level and is still largely surrounded by a ditch. Just south of the motte, crop marks have revealed the location of an oval bailey which enclosed two rectangular structures.

Historical documents imply that the motte once supported stone buildings, but, thus far, nothing has been uncovered to substantiate this notion. Post holes were noted when the site was surveyed in the late 20th century, and 13th-century potsherds were found as well. Located at the south-western side of the motte but within the bailey, the post holes may have been part of the original bridge across the ditch.

In 1215, Welsh insurgents led by Rhys Ieuanc captured and destroyed Castell Talybont during Llywelyn ab Iorwerth's rebellion against the Crown. However, the English soon regained control of the site, which was then used by the lordship of Gower. Talybont was eventually abandoned, perhaps in favour of nearby Loughor Castle, which had stone defences.

Until recently, the ruins of the medieval church of Llandeilo Talybont stood not too far from the castle, but closer to the River Loughor on the northern side of the motorway. St. Teilo's church has since been removed and reconstructed as part of St. Fagans National History Museum near Cardiff. Dating to the 13th century, St. Teilo's probably replaced an even earlier Celtic church also dedicated to the saint, who died at Llandaff in AD 566.

Talyfan
(Taliban, Tall aunt)

A large ringwork much eroded
Location: 3 miles north-east of Cowbridge (ST 021 772)
Access: A public footpath runs around the site's western side

In Ystradowen on the A4222 heading north from Cowbridge, turn right on the minor road. You want to park after about a mile, where the road makes a sharp left turn and you are faced with a long straight. You want to take the well marked footpath that is the continuation of this straight but heading in the opposite direction to the road. At the end of the first field on your right, the path turns right and soon shadows the western fringes of the castle.

If you wish to explore the castle, check with the owner at Talyfan Farm (to the left of the castle as you approach it) who is often happy to allow access. He is a mine of information about the site and will explain much about its history and the ruins. He states that, according to legislation, he is legally prohibited from clearing off the undergrowth and making repairs to the castle, which is a scheduled ancient monument, and that Cadw does not have the funds to make the necessary repairs, as they consider the castle to have only local importance. He predicts that the site will continue to decay and that the castle will inevitably disappear altogether.

Castell Talyfan once served as caput for the Siwards and the St. Quintins, who also maintained castles at Llanblethian, Llanilid, and Ystradowen, the last of which occupies a glacial ridge less than 2 miles to the north-west. Also topping a glacial hillock, Castell Talyfan is a challenge to explore, but worth the brief trek from the main roadway. A farm replaced the castle in about 1700, and much of the masonry dates to that period. The lanes leading to the castle have been well trodden by cattle, and their hoof-prints also cover much of the hilltop site.

Talyfan was one of several small lordships in the Vale of Glamorgan during the 12th and 13th centuries. Speculation exists that it was built to replace the motte castle at Ystradowen, which was never completed. Much of Talyfan's history parallels that of the St. Quintins' Castle at Llanblethian. By the middle of the 13th century, Siward family fortunes in the region faltered, and Richard de Clare, Lord of Glamorgan, took control of the castle. The Lords of Glamorgan held Castell Talyfan until the late 15th century, when it reverted to the monarchy after Jasper Tudor's death. In 1545, John Thomas Basset of Llantrithyd purchased the castle, and it has remained in private hands ever since.

Castell Talyfan stands on the flat-topped summit of Pen Talyfan. The original ditch is visible around the southern and eastern sides; a length of the outer embankment survives to the east. At one time, the ditch probably encircled most of the site, but farming activities have seriously eroded portions to the north. Along the perimeter of the summit of the mound, lengths of walling can be detected underneath the bracken. In their midst, a jumble of ruined walls marks the site of the medieval castle and also the modern farmhouse that superseded it.

Talyfan was probably an early 12th-century earth and timber stronghold. More than likely, it was a ringwork, as the slightly raised ring-bank seems to indicate. At that time, the hillock was artificially modified to create outer embankments and a ditch. Of the medieval castle, portions of the curtain wall and a small, curved section of the great keep are visible amidst the ruins of the modern farmhouse. Richard Siward may have erected these structures sometime in the mid-13th century after he designated the site as his caput.

Unfortunately due to the poor quality of the sandy mortar, only a bit of the round keep survives; in its heyday the building would have completely overawed the hilltop. Alongside the remains, remnants of another medieval building are identifiable on the north-east side of the keep. Characterised by the Royal Commission as a square annexe and an associated latrine turret, this building rises considerably higher than the lone surviving chunk of the round keep, apparently because it was constructed with better quality lime-based mortar. Except for pieces of curtain wall on the southern, northern, and eastern sides, the rest of the structures dates to the 18th and 19th centuries.

During the barons' rebellion of 1321, Castell Talyfan was attacked and burned, and its livestock slaughtered. By 1349, the site had been rebuilt and a deer park added. By the time of Leland's visit in the 1530s, the castle had fallen into ruin, but was solid enough to still hold administrative courts. In 1551, it passed to Anthony Mansel by right of marriage to Elizabeth Basset, heiress to the Basset estate. Their daughter inherited the site and passed it to her husband, Thomas Aubrey, whose family continued to own the property until the 19th century.

Tomen y Clawdd

A motte
Location: In Tonteg, 4 miles west of Caerphilly (ST 091 865)
Access: Free public access from surrounding roads
in a residential area

Take the A473 south-east from Pontypridd and, at the sweeping curve passing through Tonteg, turn right at the crossroads controlled by traffic lights. Take the first left at Fford Gerdinan, and then another immediate left. Continue to the end of the road, where the tree-topped motte is quite visible.

Originally, the circular motte overlooked the confluence of two streams, one of which may have filled the castle's moat. The broad mound still rises about 3 metres above its ditch and stretches some 21 metres across. A fairly substantial counterscarp bank rims the southern half of the mound and also continues around the north-western side. No evidence survives of an associated bailey.

While the historical record is silent about this castle, its strategic placement at the northern fringes of Meisgyn (Miskin) – where Norman territory met the Welsh-held Blaenau Glamorgan uplands – suggests a role as a frontier fortification.

226

Treoda (Whitchurch)

The site has been built over (ST 156 804)

Not only was Treoda a fine Norman motte, it was a Bronze Age burial site and probably also occupied a corner of a Roman fort. The presence of a ready-made mound, which measured 25 metres in diameter, inspired the castle's builders to place the motte on top of the burial site.

Originally located not too far north-east of St. Mary's parish church, the site no longer survives, due to Cardiff's urban sprawl in the late 20th century. Fortunately, rescue excavations in 1966 provided a record of the site and also recovered Roman-era potsherds.

The castle's basal diameter once measured about 40 metres, and the motte probably stood some 3 metres above the ditch. When G.T. Clark explored and sketched the site in 1848, he noted the truncated summit and mentioned it to a Mr. Rowland, the owner of the site, who confirmed that he had chopped almost 2 metres off the structure. Rowland apparently also filled in the ditch with spoil from the motte and used the masonry rubble to bolster his own home.

Besides speculating that the motte had at one time been taller, Clark noted the presence of an earthen rampart enclosing a rectangular area with the motte on its north-eastern side. He made no mention of a stone tower on the motte, but his later writings claim otherwise. It is likely that a stone structure of some kind stood on the site in the Middle Ages – and perhaps survived into modern times. However, by 1848, if indeed such as structure did exist, it lay underneath years of accumulated soil and vegetation. The presence of a round tower on the motte cannot now be verified, as the site has been destroyed.

Castell Treoda is listed in Gilbert de Clare III's inquisition post-mortem of 1314 and again in a royal writ dating to 1315, when Llywelyn Bren leased the site. By 1349, when it was mentioned in Hugh le Despenser's post-mortem, Treoda had been refortified. However, in the 16th century, Leland described the castle as ruinous.

227

Twmpath, Rhiwbina

A large motte
Location: On the north-western outskirts of Cardiff (ST 154 822)
Access: Can be reached by public footpath

Located close to the M4 motorway, this well preserved motte stands at the edge of Rhiwbina, in suburban Cardiff. Take the M4 to exit 32, and then head south on the A470. Pass under the M4, and, at the lights, veer left onto Pantmawr Road. Continue to the T-junction, and turn right onto Rhiwbina Hill. Next, turn left at the first large junction (Deri Inn and Deri Stores to your left). Turn left onto Brynteg, and then take a right onto Clos y Bryn. Park at road's end. Find the public footpath on the left, cross the stile, and walk ahead. The motte will appear on the left in the open field.

When originally erected at the southern end of a glacial ridge in the lordship of Whitchurch, Twmpath had all the features of a classic motte castle. Its earthen mound stood close to Cwm Nofydd and Cwm Briwnant and their bisecting streams and was strategically positioned near the River Taff, which flows about a mile to the west. Nowadays, the perimeter of the motte is engulfed by bracken and a few trees, but the interior is clear and grassy. The centre of the summit, which stretches about 15 metres in diameter, dips slightly; the depression apparently marks the spot where archaeologists dug a trench in recent decades. Around the entire base, the steep-sided ditch still protects the motte, but portions are now in-filled with bracken. There is no visible evidence of a bailey.

Like most of Glamorgan's motte castles, nothing is known of Twmpath's history. The Royal Commission speculate that, while the castle was undoubtedly a Norman creation, it may have passed to the Welsh in the mid-12th century.

Ty Du

Assorted earthwork remains
Location: 4 miles north-east of Cowbridge (ST 046 770)
Access: A public footpath passes close to the site

Head south on the minor road at Junction 34 on the M4. Turn right at the first crossroads (in Clawdd-coch), and then right again in about ¼ mile in the hamlet of Tre-Dodridge. You want to park on the left after about ½ mile when the road makes a sharp turn to the right (if you reach another road junction you've gone just too far).

A well disguised stile, to the right of a gateway which is blocked and obscured by a barbed wire and a large hunk of blackened sheet metal, leads from where you've parked into a field and you follow the hedgeline on your right away from the road and down to some woodland. Another stile leads across a stream (if you can manage it) on your right into another field. The earthworks will then lie ahead of you, half left, between you and the stream.

For some reason, certain historians doubt that the structure actually functioned as a castle mound. But a site visit will convince all comers that Ty Du was indeed a medieval castle, albeit one that rose less than 2 metres and stretched about 19 metres across the summit. The entire site is surrounded by a noticeable ditch, which is still filled by the waters of the nearby Nant Tredodridge. The open area to the north of the motte is riddled with humps and bumps, which suggest additional human activity at the site. The bailey may have been located here. Ty Du is reputedly the smallest motte in Glamorgan. Almost nothing is known of its history, except that the motte was in the lordship of Talyfan.

Tythegston Court

Some parts of the present building date back to a
13th-century tower
Location: Roughly halfway between Porthcawl and Bridgend
(SS 957 789)
Access: Private, but the 18th-century house can be partially
seen from the A4106

Even though the Royal Commission include Tythegston Court in its book on the later castles of Glamorgan, Charles Knight, the present owner, has stated, 'Tythegston cannot really be described as a castle, although some parts of the tower do date back to the 13th century. Most of the house was totally reconfigured in the 1770s by my ancestor Colonel Henry Knight.' Nowadays, Tythegston Court is a grand residence that reflects its later Tudor and Georgian heritage.

Much of what has been decided about the earlier castle derives from an interpretation of the historical record and comparisons with other tower houses, rather than from the actual examination of medieval architecture inside Tythegston Court. Fortunately, before Henry Knight began remodelling his home in the 18th century, he did document the existence of a battlemented, three-storey gabled tower.

Medieval masonry evidently survives underneath later work at the south-western corner of the property, where a substantial rectangular building stands alongside a shorter, two-storey building; both structures date to the 14th century. The taller, corner structure still contains an intact vaulted cellar and thick internal walls on all but the northern side of the ground and first floors. The two-storey annexe, which stands just north-west of the original tower house, may have functioned as a hall.

Variously known as 'Llandudwg', 'Llandudouck', and 'Landidwg' for its association with nearby St. Tudwg's parish church, and also as 'Tedegestow', 'Tegestow', and 'Tythestowe', the status of the Tythegston estate was raised to a sub-manor in the late 13th century. In about 1300, Wilcock Turberville acquired the tower house, and the Turbervilles held the property until the 1530s, when heiress Gwenllian Turberville passed it by right of marriage to her husband, Watkin Lougher. Gwenllian's cousin, Christopher Turberville, contested Lougher's rights to the tower house. The legal battle that ensued was not settled until 1546, when Gwenllian finally received Tythegston and lands at Newton Nottage, and Christopher acquired Penllyn and North Cornelly.

According to the historical record, the Loughers rebuilt the tower house at Tythegston in the mid-16th century. It remained in their hands until the early 18th century, when Cecil Turberville, the granddaughter of Richard Lougher, inherited the site after her mother died in 1701. Seven years later, when Cecil married Robert Knight, Tythegston manor house passed to the family whose descendant, Charles H. Knight, still owns the property. Colonel Henry Knight occupied Tythegston Court from 1765-72. During this time the house underwent its greatest transformation; most of the present structure dates to this period.

Walterston

Little physical evidence remains
Location: 3 miles north-west of Barry (ST 068 712)
Access: Nothing can be seen from the adjacent roads

North of the road junction in the hamlet of the same name, the banks of a large partial ringwork are said to survive alongside a small brook at Walterston. Although historical documents do not mention the castle, they do record the name 'A. de Waltervilla', who probably founded the site, perhaps as a settlement, in about 1102. A farmhouse named Trewallter Fawr implies proximity to the ringwork.

During a site survey in the 1970s, archaeologists described the ringwork as a 'strongly embanked enclosure', the northern side of which was heavily defended with a strong bank and ditch. The embankment stretched 50 metres from the brook on the east around to the western side, portions of which have been destroyed. Foundations of a small rectangular stone structure and fragments of 12th-century pottery were discovered during the excavations, when archaeologists also noted a much larger, circular embankment to the north and west of the ringwork. The Royal Commission speculate that it may have enclosed de Waltervilla's 12th-century settlement rather than the castle's bailey.

Walterston is best reached from the A4226, which leads south from the A48 at Sycamore Cross. After about 1¼ miles, head west toward Walterston. The ringwork stood to the right (north) at the main junction in the centre of Walterston.

Weobley

Substantial stonework remains
Location: West of Llanrhidian in north Gower (SS 478 928)
Access: Managed by Cadw and open at reasonable times for a fee

Take the B4295 westward along the northern side of the Gower, heading through Llanrhidian and thence in the direction of Cheriton. A short lane to the right leads to the castle car park.

Poised to overlook marshland known as Llanrhidian Sands, which is adjacent to the River Loughor, Weobley is the lone stone castle on the northern side of the Gower Peninsula. Owain Glyndwr conducted the only attack of consequence on the structure, which was really a fortified manor house. His assault in 1403 essentially destroyed the site, but it was promptly rebuilt and used for several more centuries.

In the early 13th century, John de Turberville, Lord of Coity, granted to David de la Bere the right to establish a minor lordship, or fee, in the area. Variously known as 'Weobley', 'Webley', or

'Webbley', and also as 'Leyston' or 'Leysanteston', the site served as the fee's caput. (Leyston is associated with Leason, a nearby farm; remnants of the medieval settlement no longer survive.) The origins of the Weobley name are uncertain; however, the de la Bere family did have connections with the Herefordshire Weobleys and it is possible that the Welsh castle takes its name from that family.

David de la Bere, who served as Swansea Castle's steward in 1292, probably first established a ringwork castle either at Cil Ifor, just east of Weobley Castle, or at North Hill Tor, just to the west. Earthworks survive at both sites and are described elsewhere in this book. Later in the 13th century, the de la Bere family moved their family seat to the stone castle/manor house. John St. John, whose family owned Fonmon Castle in the Vale of Glamorgan, obtained a grant for Weobley Castle when John de la Bere died in 1403. Lleucu Bassett, St. John's wife, gained control of the Weobley estates in the mid-15th century, and, for a time, leased the castle to Richard Lougher. Weobley Castle and its estates eventually passed to Lady Lleucu's nephew, Sir Rhys ap Thomas.

The fortified manor house is a rarity in Wales, and Weobley Castle is one of the finest examples of its type. The design actually reflects two building phases, both of which occurred in the 14th century but were initiated by different owners. The oldest buildings include the large south-western tower, the hall block on the northern side of the castle, and portions of the east range.

Standing offset from the line created with the construction of the gatehouse during a later building phase, the massive two-storey south-western tower was initially a freestanding structure entered by a doorway at first-floor level. Possibly been intended as a keep, only the lowest foundations survive to any degree. Its 12-metre thick walls would have posed a considerable barrier to an enemy attack. A cistern tower projects outward from the western side of the south-western tower. A deep pit (the cistern) in the tower's basement collected and stored rainwater and supplied residents with a fairly stable source of drinking water. Weobley Castle apparently never had a well.

The chapel block stands in an advanced state of ruin to the east of the south-western tower. Once an eye-catching building, the structure still contains a 14th-century piscina and some notable carvings, including a fireplace head and a trefoil window. Like the gatehouse (see below), the chapel building filled a gap in the walling, but it also played an essential role in the daily life of the residents.

On the northern side of the gravely courtyard opposite the chapel is the hall block, arguably the most impressive range in the castle. The elaborate porchway added by Sir Rhys ap Thomas in the late 15th century is one of the hall's finest features. Inside, all visitors first stepped into a barrel-vaulted antechamber; anyone wanting an audience with the lord would wait here until being beckoned into the great hall. The chamber to the east provided access to the eastern range and also to service rooms alongside the kitchen.

The 14th-century hall block was actually built in two phases. Initially, the building behind the porchway held a combined hall-and-kitchen block on the ground floor. During the second phase, the great hall was lifted to the upper storey and the entire lower level became the kitchen. It featured a drain in the central splayed window, a small round-backed fireplace, and also a larger great fireplace. The windows had seats and could be barricaded with iron grilles and shutters.

From the great hall, guests could admire the panorama of Llanrhidian Sands. The impressive chamber measured an enormous 11.4 metres by 6.7 metres. Its elaborate cinquefoil-headed windows were mullioned and had socket-holes for barring. At the far end, the dais once supported the lord's table. A recess in the wall behind the dais may have been used to hang tapestries or panelling to impress the guests. A doorway allowed access to the solar, which occupied the castle's north-westernmost corner. The solar still contains an impressive first-floor fireplace, mullioned windows with seats, and access to a private garderobe.

Built during the second building phase to fill the gap between the hall and the south-western tower, the simple gatehouse essentially linked the solar to the tower. Consisting mainly of an archway defended only by wooden gates placed at the outer side of the gate passage, the poorly defended gatehouse even lacked the standard portcullis and arrowslits; rather than bolstering the defences, the meagre ditch along the exterior side of the gatehouse was probably dug to provide a convenient source of limestone. (It would have been burned to make mortar in the kiln at the eastern end of the castle.) The upper storey of the gatehouse offered accommodation and shared a latrine with the solar. Its most notable features include splayed windows with seats, a round-backed fireplace, and socket-holes for an iron grille.

The castle's easternmost end is also its most ruinous, primarily because it was never fully completed. The covered wall-walk, which occupied the area between the hall block and the east range, held three garderobes and also provided access into a separate latrine turret on the north-eastern corner of the east range. Only the northernmost portion of the eastern range was finished – a cross-wall marks the point where construction halted. The two-storey building contained fireplaces, trefoil and quatrefoil windows, and easy access to garderobes, one of which still retains its stone seat. Originally, the chute emptied into a cesspit and its contents then slid outside the castle walls.

The eastern range also contains a curious winding structure, which protrudes from the ground alongside the limekiln and is best viewed from outside the castle. The remnants of what would have been the square south-eastern tower are now severely degraded. In fact, only the lowest foundations and a sturdy angle-spur were ever completed. Remains of three latrine chutes are visible, however. To the north of the tower, the southern part of the eastern range still contains an oven, fireplace, and drain; the basement level would have functioned as a bakehouse and kitchen. This area of the castle probably held guest accommodation or housed servants.

In 1531, Rhys ap Gruffydd, grandson of Rhys ap Thomas, was convicted of committing treason and executed for his crimes. Consequently, Weobley Castle reverted to the monarchy. In 1560, Queen Elizabeth I sold the castle to William Herbert, Earl of Pembroke, whose heirs leased it to various tenants, including Rowland Vaughan of Pembrey. William Seys was the tenant in 1666 when the Herberts finally sold the castle to Sir Edward Mansel of Margam. Weobley Castle then passed by right of marriage from the Mansels to the Talbots, whose heiress, Emily Charlotte Talbot, placed the castle in the care of the State in 1911.

Ynyscrug
(Rhondda Castle)

Traces of a motte remain (SS 995 928)
Location: By the side of the new line of the A4058
Access: Free access

The few traces that do exist are located near Trealaw, east of
Tonypandy and on the eastern side of the River Rhondda where
it converges with the Clydach. The new line of the A4058 passes
close by, and the remains are near the new 'Ynyscrug' roundabout.

In 1855, construction of the Taff Vale Railway partially obliterated the earthwork castle. Poised to overlook the confluence of
the Rivers Rhondda and Clydach, the motte and bailey may have
been the manorial centre of Glynrhondda in the Welsh lordship of
Meisgyn (Miskin). In 1245, Richard de Clare probably annexed the
site, along with much of the rest of the lordship.

Like other motte castles in the Vale of Glamorgan, Castell
Ynyscrug stood on a hill of glacial drift. Only the western side
survives close to the railway; the bailey was destroyed by roadworks in 1986.

Ystradowen

Large motte
Location: 2 miles north-west of Cowbridge (ST 011 777)
Access: Free public access

Travellers heading south toward Cowbridge on the A4222 will find themselves suddenly thrust into the middle of Ystradowen, a pleasant village flanking both sides of the roadway. Just behind the White Lion pub on the south side of Ystradowen, the slender tower on the village church points the way to the one of Glamorgan's more unusual mottes. Ystradowen Castle occupies land immediately adjacent to the church of St. Owain.

Second only to Cardiff Castle in diameter at 47 metres, Ystradowen Castle's tree-topped motte sits in the midst of an open field. Its builders were probably either the St. Quintin family or their rivals, the Siwards, who held nearby Llanblethian and Talyfan castles in the early 12th century. They would have chosen this particular site due to its natural advantages, most notably, the presence of a glacial hump which only needed shaping to become a useful castle mound. Some historians speculate that the castle may have been the predecessor to Talyfan, which became the caput for the area; this shift of roles may explain why Ystradowen Castle was never finished.

The more-or-less round motte is still largely surrounded by a dry ditch. The north-western side of the castle is actually level with the field beyond, which would have been the most difficult part of the site for medieval labourers to excavate. A hollowed-out area dominates the summit, which extends about 20 metres in diameter. Earth dug from the spot was piled on the summit's western side. The castle builders may have intended to raise the mound even higher, or perhaps, to construct a ring-bank, as the presence of the pile and crater seem to suggest. In any event, they never completed the task. It should be noted that, if the original intent was to add a ring-bank, Ystradowen should be classified as a ringwork.

First documented in the 12th century, the adjacent church was last restored in the 1860s. Local tradition says that Owain, son of a 12th-century king of Glamorgan, built both the church and the castle and was later buried here along with his wife. In the late 19th or early 20th century, antiquarians decided to excavate what they believed to be 'King Owen's' burial mound to carry off whatever treasure might have been buried there seven hundred years earlier. Sadly, all they managed to do was damage the southeastern side of the motte.

Further Reading

Davies, RR. *The Age of Conquest: Wales 1063-1415.* Oxford University Press, 1991.

Friend, Tony. *Lord Tredegar's Ruperra Castle.* Newport Local History Society, 1986.

Glenn, Charles. *The Lords of Cardiff Castle.* Christopher Davies (Publishers) Ltd, 1976.

Grant, John P. *Cardiff Castle: its history and architecture.* William Lewis (Printers) Ltd, 1923.

Grenfell, Harold E and Bernard Morris. *The Castles of the Gower.* Gower Society, 1985.

Maund, Kari. *The Welsh Kings: the medieval rulers of Wales.* Tempus Publishing Ltd, 2000.

Newman, John. *Glamorgan (Mid Glamorgan, South Glamorgan and West Glamorgan).* Penguin Books Ltd, 1995.

Nicholas, Thomas. *The History and Antiquities of Glamorganshire and its Families.* Stewart Williams, 1970.

Pugh, TB, ed. *Glamorgan County History, Volume III, The Middle Ages, The Marcher Lordships of Glamorgan and Morgannwg & Gower and Kilvey from the Norman Conquest to the Act of Union.* University of Wales Press, 1971.

Rees, William. *Caerphilly Castle and its Place in the Annals of Glamorgan.* Caerphilly Local History Society, 1978.

Renn, Derek. *Caerphilly Castle.* Cadw: Welsh Historic Monuments, 1997.

Richard, Arthur J. 'The Castles of Glamorgan: An Introductory Study', in *Glamorgan Historian*, volume one, pp 37-43, 1963.

Salter, Mike. *The Castles of Gwent, Glamorgan & Gower.* Folly Publications, 1991.

Spurgeon, CJ. 'Supposed Castles in Glamorgan: a review', in *Archaeology in Wales*: 39, 1999.

The Royal Commission on the Ancient and Historical Monuments of Wales. *An Inventory of the Ancient Monuments in Glamorgan, Volume III - Part Ib: Medieval Secular Monuments, The Later Castles from 1217 to the Present.* HMSO, 2000.

The Royal Commission on Ancient and Historical Monuments in Wales. *An Inventory of the Ancient Monuments in Glamorgan, Volume III - Part Ia: Medieval Secular Monuments, The Early Castles from the Norman Conquest to 1217.* HMSO, 1991.

The Royal Commission on Ancient and Historical Monuments in Wales. *An Inventory of the Ancient Monuments in Glamorgan, Volume III - Part II: Medieval Secular Monuments, Non-defensive.* HMSO, 1982.

The Royal Commission on Ancient and Historical Monuments in Wales. *An Inventory of the Ancient Monuments in Glamorgan, Volume IV: Domestic Architecture from the Reformation to the Industrial Revolution, Part I: The Greater Houses.* HMSO, 1981.

Walker, David. *Medieval Wales.* Cambridge University Press, 1990.

Whittle, Elizabeth. *A Guide to Ancient and Historic Wales: Glamorgan and Gwent.* HMSO, 1992.

Williams, Diane M. *Gower: A Guide to Ancient and Historic Monuments on the Gower Peninsula.* Cadw: Welsh Historic Monuments, 1998.

Glossary of Terms

abutment: solid masonry placed to counteract the lateral thrust of a bridge, arch, or vault

angle-spur: pyramid-shaped projections rising at the corners of towers, intended for added support and to prevent collapse from undermining

arrowslit: narrow, vertical slit in castle walls used for firing arrows from inside castle; also called 'arrowloop'

ashlar: building stone neatly trimmed to shape; stone with cut flat surface

attainder: forfeiture of hereditary honours and dignities following a conviction for treason

aumbry: a mural cupboard for storing valuables

bailey: defended courtyard or ward of a castle; open area enclosed by the castle walls; a ward

barbican: fortified outwork defending the gate of a castle or town

barrel vault: a vault in the shape of a half barrel split lengthways

batter: inward and upward slope of an external wall, normally located at its base

berm: flat area between the base of a wall and edge of a ditch or moat

bratticing: wooden housing erected on top of walls; known as 'war-head' when erected on towers; see 'hoarding'

buttery: storeroom where wine and other drink were dispensed from barrels, the 'bottlery'; usually located between the hall and the kitchen

buttress: thickening of a wall or projecting masonry, added for strength and support

cantref: Welsh administrative unit of land division

capital: head of a column

caput: feudal term for the administrative centre of a lordship

castellation: battlements; implies use as a decorative feature

chamfer: bevelled face formed by cutting off the corner of stone or timber structure; the plane formed when the sharp edge or angle of a squared stone block is cut away

chancery: medieval high court which presided over cases of common law and equity; chancellor's court or office

chemise: a masonry wall situated to protect the base of a keep or a tower, a wall set a few metres before the structure it is defending, as at Penrice Castle

concentric: having two parallel lines of defence, the lower outer wall closely surrounding the higher inner; a walls-within-walls design; circles within circles

comitatus: county court

constable: governor of a castle

corbel: projecting stone (or timber) feature on a wall to support an
   overhanging parapet, platform, turret, or timber beams

counterscarp: outer slope of a defensive ditch

crenellation: toothlike protective stonework rimming the top of a castle wall;
   fortification, including crenels and merlons; a 'license to crenellate' was
   official permission from the monarch to raise a fortified building or fortify
   an existing structure

cross-wall: a stone wall that creates a barrier between two chambers or forms
   part of a passageway between two structures

crosslet/crosslit: a loophole arranged in the form of a cross; also called 'cross-
   oillet'

curtain: defensive wall which encloses a bailey, courtyard, or ward, generally
   constructed in stone; links towers, the main gateway, and other structures

custodian: manager of castle in absence of lord

dais: a raised platform for the high table, at the end of the great hall, where
   the lord and his guests dined

demesne: land retained and used by the lord

D-plan: semicircular design of towers, often indicates a castle's Welsh-built
   origins; apsidal

drawbar: sliding wooden bar to secure a door in the closed position

dressed stone: stone worked into a smooth or moulded face; used to outline
   angles, windows, and doors

drum tower: a completely round tower

drystone: method of building without mortar or clay

embrasure: splayed opening in a wall or parapet; arrow loops cut into the
   merlons

enceinte: enclosure or courtyard wall

fee: land held by a knight or other landowner in exchange for the military
   service of a single knight

feudalism: a political and economic system under which land was granted by
   a landowner to a person in exchange for military service or other duties

forebuilding: projecting defensive work that screens the entrance to keep or
   other structures and guards from direct attack

freestone: stone that is easily cut and moulded, such as fine grained limestone
   or sandstone

garderobe: usually the latrine chute, privy, or castle toilet; sometimes, a room
   to store personal items, a wardrobe

hoarding: wooden fighting platform fitted to the parapet of wall as extra
   protection for defenders and to offer an additional area from which to fire
   down on an enemy

hornwork: outer earthwork barrier usually set before an entrance to impede
   attackers

inner ward: interior courtyard, hub of castle where daily activities took place

Ionic: style of Greek capital that features scrolls at either end

jamb: vertical side of a doorway, window, archway, or fireplace

keep: the main citadel or great tower of a castle; a fortified tower containing living quarters and used as the last line of refuge in a siege; a self-sufficient tower; the 'donjon'

keystone: central wedge-shaped stone at the top of an arch

lancet-headed: pointed arches at peaks of narrow windows

latrine chute: an open channel in a tower or wall through which human waste passes into a cesspit or outside the castle walls into the moat

machicolation: openings in the floor of a projecting parapet or platform, located along a wall or above an archway, through which defenders could drop or shoot missiles vertically onto attackers below; functioned similar to murder holes

marches: borderlands or frontier, especially associated with the border between Wales and England

merlon: the 'teeth' of battlements, rising between the crenels or embrasures; high sections of battlement

motte: artificial or improved natural mound on which a timber tower or shell keep was built

mullion: vertical bar of stone or wood dividing a window into smaller openings

mural stairs: stone stairs rising in the wall

murderholes: openings in the ceilings of gate passages, through which missiles and liquids could be dropped onto attackers or fires

newel stair: circular or spiral stair within a wall or tower; treads radiating from a central post or column are called a 'newel'

oillet: an eye hole; roundel at the end of a cross-shaped arrow loop

oratory: a small private chamber for prayer

oriel: a large projecting, curved, or polygonal window supported on corbels

oubliette: tiny cell where prisoners were left to die; secret chamber; pit prison

plinth: projecting platforms of heavy stone upon which keeps or wall towers were raised to prevent undermining

portcullis: heavy wooden, iron, or combination grille protecting an entrance; raised and lowered by winches (the windlass) located inside the gatehouse; grooves visible in many gate passages

postern: secondary gateway or back doorway, used for quick escape or to take in supplies

putlog holes: square holes left by the withdrawal of timbers being used as scaffolding

quatrefoil: four-lobed or four-leaved

quoins: stones, frequently dressed, used to form the angles of buildings or walls

relieving arch: roughly constructed false arch

revetment: an outwork or embankment faced with a layer of timber or
    masonry for added strength and to avoid erosion, particularly useful in the
    ditch

ringwork: an earth and timber fortification similar to a motte but where the
    summit is dished to some degree, encircled with earthen banks, which
    were then topped with timber palisades

sallyport: small door or gate, usually some distance from main entrance of
    castle or ward, often hidden to allow defenders to enter and exit castle
    without detection and surprise attackers; related to 'sally forth'

scarp: the inner slope of a defensive ditch; an artificially-cut slope constructed
    for defence

shell keep: a ring of stone wall encircling the top of a motte, which held
    domestic chambers, the hall, and other facilities

slighting: the process of rendering a castle useless to prevent its future use;
    dismantling a fortification accomplished by breaching walls, undermining
    walls, and, later, by blowing them up with gun powder; a policy enforced
    by Oliver Cromwell to ensure all castles were unable to oppose his
    authority after the English Civil War

solar: private living quarters of lord, usually adjacent to great hall; a
    withdrawing chamber

splay: an aperture that widens as it progresses inwards, normally associated
    with windows

springer: the portion of an arch, vault, or set of stones closest to the vertical
    column to which the arch or vault is attached

steward: individual who took care of the estate and supervised the castle's
    household and events in the great hall; also known as a 'seneschal'

string course: horizontal projecting moulding or band of masonry running
    along the face of a wall

tower house: a significantly fortified residence built to thwart brief assaults
    rather than prolonged sieges; architecturally similar to a rectangular keep

tracery: decorative, curving stonework commonly used on windows

transom: horizontal bar of stone or wood that divided the lights in a window

trefoil: three-lobed or three-leaved, often associated with window design

undercroft: plain room underneath a medieval house or castle, most often
    used as storage and barrel-vaulted

vault: an arched roof, usually of stone

wall-walk: interior walkway along a wall top, protected by a parapet

ward: courtyard or confined bailey enclosed within castle walls